D1710761

Common Corporate Tax Base (CC(C)TB)
and Determination of Taxable Income

Christoph Spengel • York Zöllkau
Editors

Common Corporate Tax Base (CC(C)TB) and Determination of Taxable Income

An International Comparison

 Springer

Editors
Professor Dr. Christoph Spengel
University of Mannheim and Centre
for European Economic Research (ZEW)
Mannheim
Germany

York Zöllkau
Ernst & Young GmbH
Wirtschaftsprüfungsgesellschaft
Cologne
Germany

ISBN 978-3-642-28432-8   e-ISBN 978-3-642-28433-5
DOI 10.1007/978-3-642-28433-5
Springer Heidelberg Dordrecht London New York

Library of Congress Control Number: 2012934150

Printed on acid-free paper

Springer is part of Springer Science+Business Media (www.springer.com)

Preface

After intensive and extensive preparation, the European Commission released the awaited proposal for a Council Directive on a Common Consolidated Corporate Tax Base (CCCTB) on March 16, 2011. The CCCTB is a proposal to provide companies with the opportunity to determine taxable income following a three-step approach: (1) Determination of individual income based on a harmonised set of tax accounting regulations, (2) consolidation of individual incomes and (3) allocation of the consolidated tax base by formula apportionment.

Yet, as the second and third step of a CCCTB, i.e. the consolidation and the sharing mechanism, still suffer from considerable shortcomings, we recommend introducing the CCCTB in two steps. The first step merely concerns the replacement of the national tax accounting regulations across Member States by a single set of harmonised tax rules. Such a Common Corporate Tax Base (CCTB) only affects the calculation of the corporate tax base; the consolidation and allocation of the common tax base would be omitted for the present and considered at a later stage of tax harmonisation in Europe.

Our study contributes to the ongoing evaluation of the proposed Council Directive. For the first time, details on the determination of taxable income under the proposed Council Directive are being compared and contrasted to prevailing corporate tax accounting regulations as of January 1, 2011 in all 27 Member States, Switzerland and the US. In doing so, we present evidence on the extent of differences and similarities between national tax accounting regulations and the Directive's treatment in a complete, yet concise form.

The study was conducted by a research consortium of Ernst & Young (EY)[1], the Centre for European Economic Research (ZEW) and the University of Mannheim. The detailed information on national tax accounting regulations in the 29 countries under consideration were compiled and provided by the Ernst & Young member firms in the respective countries. The ZEW and the University of Mannheim were responsible for the description of the proposed Council Directive and the comparative analysis.

---

[1] In this publication, "Ernst & Young" and "we" refer to all member firms of Ernst & Young Global Limited. Neither Ernst & Young Germany nor any other member of the global Ernst & Young organization can accept any responsibility. On any specific matter, reference should be made to appropriate advisor.

We are grateful to all EY country contributors, who completed the questionnaire underlying this study. We owe our gratitude to Maria-Theresia Evers, Marcel Olbert and Stefanie Stohn for research assistance and to Henrik Schoch and Nadine Weinhauer for editorial work.

Christoph Spengel
University of Mannheim and ZEW
Mannheim

York Zöllkau
Ernst & Young GmbH
Cologne

Mannheim and Cologne, January 2012

Content

List of Figures

List of Tables

Abbreviations

AT	Austria
BE	Belgium
BG	Bulgaria
CC(C)TB	Common Corporate (Consolidated) Tax Base
CD	Council Directive
CFC	Controlled Foreign Company
CH	Switzerland
CY	Cyprus
CZ	Czech Republic
DE	Germany
DK	Denmark
EBIT	Earnings Before Interest and Taxes
EBITDA	Earnings Before Interest, Taxes, Depreciation and Amortisation
EEA	European Economic Area
EEAA	European Economic Area Agreement
EE	Estonia
ES	Spain
EU	European Union
EUR	Euro
Euribor	Euro Interbank Offered Rate
EY	Ernst & Young
FI	Finland
FiFo	First In, First Out
FR	France
GAAP	Generally Accepted Accounting Principles
GR	Greece
HiFo	Highest In, First Out
HU	Hungary
IAS	International Accounting Standards
IBFD	International Bureau for Fiscal Documentation
IE	Ireland
IFRS	International Financial Reporting Standards
IT	Italy
LiFo	Last In, First Out
LT	Lithuania
LU	Luxembourg
LV	Latvia
MT	Malta
NL	the Netherlands
OECD	Organisation for Economic Co-operation and Development

p(p).	page(s)
PL	Poland
PT	Portugal
R&D	Research and Development
RO	Romania
SE	Sweden
SI	Slovenia
SL	Slovakia
SLR	Straight-line Rate
UK	United Kingdom
UL	Useful Life
US	United States of America
ZEW	Centre for European Economic Research (ZEW), Mannheim

Authors

Professor Dr. Christoph Spengel
University of Mannheim
Business School (BSUM) and ZEW
Schloss, Ostflügel
68131 Mannheim
spengel@uni-mannheim.de

Martina Ortmann-Babel, StB
Ernst & Young GmbH
Wirtschaftsprüfungsgesellschaft
Mittlerer Pfad 15
70499 Stuttgart
martina.ortmann@de.ey.com

Sebastian Matenaer
University of Mannheim Business
School (BSUM)
Schloss, Ostflügel
68131 Mannheim
matenaer@uni-mannheim.de

York Zöllkau, StB / WP
Ernst & Young GmbH
Wirtschaftsprüfungsgesellschaft
Ludwigstrasse 8
50667 Cologne
york.zoellkau@de.ey.com

Benedikt Zinn
Centre for European Economic Research
(ZEW)
L7,1
68161 Mannheim
zinn@zew.de

Janine von Wolfersdorff
Cologne
von_wolfersdorff@ifst.de

Country Contributions

Coordination: Dr. Klaus von Brocke, Head of EU Tax Network
Ernst & Young GmbH Wirtschaftsprüfungsgesellschaft,
Arnulfstrasse 59, 80636 München

Roland Rief
Ernst & Young, Austria
Ernst & Young Steuerberatungs- und
Wirtschaftsprüfungsgesellschaft m.b.H.
Wagramer Str. 19
1220 Vienna

Steven J Claes
Ernst & Young, Belgium
Ernst & Young
De Kleetlaan 2
B1831 Diegem

Trevor Link
Ernst & Young, Bulgaria
Ernst & Young Bulgaria
EOOD
Polygrahia Office Center, Fourth Floor
Tsarigradsko shoes blvd 47A
1124 Sofia

Maarten Koper
Ernst & Young, Cyprus
Ernst & Young Cyprus Limited
27-29 Spyrou Kyprianou Avenue
Mesa Geitonia
4003 Limassol

Libor Fryzek
Ernst & Young, Czech Republic
Ernst & Young, s.r.o.
Karlovo nam.10
120 00 Praha 2

Martina Ortmann-Babel
Ernst & Young, Germany
Ernst & Young GmbH
Wirtschaftsprüfungsgesellschaft
Mittlerer Pfad 15
70499 Stuttgart

Leonas Lingis
Ernst & Young, Lithuania
Ernst & Young Baltic UAB
Subaciaus 7
Vilnius LT-01127

Anja Taferner
Ernst & Young, Luxembourg
Ernst & Young LLP
5 Times Square, New York
NY 10036

Christopher Naudi
Ernst & Young, Malta
Ernst & Young Limited
Fourth Floor
Regional Business Centre
Achille Ferris Street Msida MSD 1751
Malta

Arjo van Eijsden
Ernst & Young, the Netherlands
Ernst & Young Belastingadviseurs LLP
P.O. Box 2295
3000 CG Rottderdam

Andrzej Broda
Ernst & Young, Poland
Ernst & Young Sp. z.o.o.
Rondo ONZ 1
00-124 Warszawa

Antonio Neves
Ernst & Young, Portugal
Ernst & Young
Avenida da República
90 - 3 Andar
1649-024 Lisbon

Niels Josephsen
Ernst & Young, Denmark
Ernst & Young P/S
Gyngemose parkvej 50
2860 Søborg

Ranno Tingas
Ernst & Young, Estonia
Ernst & Young Baltic AS
Rävala 4
10143 Tallinn

Katri Nygård
Ernst & Young, Finland
Ernst & Young Oy
Elielinaukio 5 B
00100 Helsinki

Anne Colmet Daâge
Ernst & Young, France
Ernst & Young Société d'Avocats
Tour Ernst & Young – Faubourg de
l'Arche
92037 Paris La Défense Cedex

Stefanos Mitsios
Ernst & Young, Greece
Ernst & Young Business Advisory
Solutions
11th km National Road Athens – Lamia
14451, Metamorphossi Athens

Balazs Szolgyemy
Ernst & Young, Hungary
Ernst & Young Advisory Ltd.
Váci út 20
1132 Budapest

Kevin McLoughlin
Ernst & Young, Ireland
Ernst & Young
Ernst & Young Building
Harcourt Street
Dublin 2

Alexander Milcev
Ernst & Young, Romania
Ernst & Young SRL
Dr. Iacob Felix 63-69
Bucharest

Denes Szabo
Ernst & Young, Slovenia
Ernst & Young Svetovanje, d.o.o./
Ernst & Young Advisory, Ltd
Dunajska cesta 111
1000 Ljubljana

Stan Jakubek
Ernst & Young, Slovakia
Ernst & Young, k.s.
Hodzovo namestie 1A
811 06, Bratislava

Carlos Gabarró
Ernst & Young, Spain
Ernst & Young Abogados, SL
Avda. Sarria, 102-106
08017 Barcelona

Erik Hultman
Ernst & Young, Sweden
Ernst & Young AB
Jakobsbergsgatan 24
P.O. Box 7850
SE-103 99 Stockholm

René Schreiber
Ernst & Young, Switzerland
Ernst & Young AG
Belpstrasse 23
P.O. Box
3001 Bern

David Evans
Ernst & Young, United Kingdom
Ernst & Young LLP
1 More London Place
London SE1 2AF

Domenico Serranó
Ernst & Young, Italy
Ernst & Young
Studio Legal Tributario
Via Della Chiusa 2
20123 Milano

Ilona Butane
Ernst & Young, Latvia
Ernst Young Baltic SIA
Muitas iela 1
Riga
LV-1010

Tom S. Neubig
Ernst & Young, United States of America
Ernst & Young LLP
1101 New York Avenue, NW
Washington, DC 20005

Executive Summary

Draft Council Directive on a Common Consolidated Corporate Tax Base (CCCTB)

On March 16, 2011, the European Commission released the awaited proposal for a Council Directive on a Common Consolidated Corporate Tax Base (CCCTB) for the taxation of the EU-wide activities of multinationals. In short, the proposed CCCTB would imply a three-step approach for the determination of taxable income:

(1) Determination of corporate taxable income of group members based on a harmonised set of tax accounting regulations;
(2) Consolidation of the individual, i.e. the group members', corporate tax bases to the common tax base;
(3) Allocation of the consolidated tax base to group members located in different Member States by formula apportionment.

Each Member State would still preserve its right to tax the allocated share of the consolidated tax base applying its own national corporate tax rate.

Although the comprehensive and coherent solution of a CCCTB as proposed by the Commission seems to be a promising avenue to reduce tax distortions in Europe in the long-run, there are considerable shortcomings at present that require further investigation. These shortcomings mainly refer to the second and the third step of a CCCTB, i.e. the consolidation and allocation of the tax base. Examples include transitional rules for the entry and exit of group members, the treatment of *third-country* relations and the consideration of intangible assets in the sharing mechanism. In this respect, further discussion and consideration, which is not likely to be available within the near future, seems necessary to fully understand and evaluate the consequences of any consolidation and sharing mechanism and convince Member States that the gains from harmonisation are worth the costs of giving up sovereignty in corporate tax policy.

The European Commission and Member States should, therefore, consider a strategy that would introduce the CCCTB in two steps. The first step comprises the replacement of the 27 national tax accounting regulations across Member States by a single set of harmonised tax rules. This Common Corporate Tax Base (CCTB) would merely affect the calculation of the corporate tax base. The second step, i.e. the consolidation of individual group members' income and the subsequent allocation of the consolidated tax base by formula apportionment, would be omitted for the present and considered at a later stage.

Objective of the Study

Against this background, the study focuses on the first salient feature of a CCCTB, i.e. the common corporate tax base (CCTB). For the first time, details on the determination of taxable income under the proposed Council Directive are compared to prevailing corporate tax accounting regulations in all 27 Member States, Switzerland and the US. More precisely, we contribute to the ongoing evaluation of the proposed Council Directive and the concept of a CCCTB by analysing whether the CCTB as established by the proposed Council Directive is appropriate to replace current national tax accounting rules in the Member States.

In doing so, Ernst & Young (EY) tax experts in all 29 considered countries have been asked to provide detailed information on the fundamental concepts of tax accounting, the recognition of revenue and expenses and the loss relief under the national tax codes currently in practice. In detail, EY members firms in the respective countries have received and responded to a jointly developed questionnaire that includes more than 80 questions concerning all important matters regulated by the proposed Council Directive. The information provided allow for a detailed and comprehensive comparison of the CCTB and the rules on the determination of corporate taxable income across Member States as of January 1, 2011.

Structure of the Study

Section B briefly reviews the current state of the CCCTB project, provides an overview of the proposed Council Directive and discusses some important advantages and questions raised by the proposal. Section C focuses on the comparative analysis of the corporate tax base regulations under the proposed Council Directive and current tax practice in all 27 EU Member States, Switzerland and the US. It systematically discusses the individual regulations, compares them in an international setting and identifies elements of the tax base which are not explicitly addressed by the proposed Council Directive. Subsequently the most important differences between the proposed Council Directive and national tax accounting regulations are summarised in Section D. Moreover, the main areas that are not covered by the proposed Council Directive or should be addressed in more detail are identified and separately presented. Finally, Section E summarises the main results.

Results of Comparative Analyses (see Sections C and D.1)

The proposed Council Directive provides a carefully prepared and comprehensive framework for the determination of corporate taxable income. Overall, the proposed rules are in line with international standards and commonly accepted principles of tax accounting and can be expected to reach consensus in the EU. Nevertheless, current Member States' tax accounting practices obviously deviate from the proposed set of autonomous tax accounting rules under a CCCTB in several ways.

Table E-1 provides an overview of these deviations and specifies whether they constitute major or minor differences between the proposed Council Directive and current tax accounting practice in the 27 EU Member States, Switzerland and the US. To this end, not only the number of countries deviating from the proposed Council Directive is taken into consideration, but attention is also paid to the significance of differences.

Table E-1: Summary of the Comparative Analyses: Proposed Council Directive on a CCCTB and Current Tax Accounting Practice in the 27 EU Member States, Switzerland and the US

Selected Issues of the Proposed Council Directive	Article	Deviation from Current Practice in the 27 EU Member States, Switzerland and the US	
		Major	Minor
Fundamental Concepts and General Principles			
Determination of the Tax Base: Starting Point			
Autonomous Tax Law	Explanatory Memorandum	✓	
Profit and Loss Account Approach	Article 10		✓
Basic Principles Underlying the Determination of the Tax Base			
Realisation Principle (Applied)	Article 9 (1)		✓
Item-by-Item Principle (Applied)	Article 9 (2)		✓
Consistency Requirement (Applied)	Article 9 (3)		✓
Anti-abuse Regulation (Applied)	Article 80		✓
Revenue			
Timing of Revenue			
General Principle (Accrual Principle)	Article 17 / 18		✓
Sales (Economic Ownership)	Article 17 / 18		✓
Profit Distributions (Dividend Resolution)	Article 17 / 18		✓
Interest (Accrual Basis)	Article 17 / 18		✓
Unrealised Revenue (Generally not Taxed)	Article 17 / 18		✓
Exceptions from the General Realisation Principle			
Financial Assets and Liabilities held for Trading (Taxed)	Article 23	✓	
Long-Term Contracts (Percentage-of-Completion)	Article 24		✓
Controlled Foreign Company (Applicable)	Article 82		✓

Selected Issues of the Proposed Council Directive	Article	Deviation from Current Practice in the 27 EU Member States, Switzerland and the US	
		Major	Minor
Taxation of Capital Gains			
General Principle (Taxable without Relief)	Article 4 (8)		✓
Replacement Assets (Rollover Relief)	Article 38	✓	
Exempt Revenue (Exempt Amount in Brackets)			
Profit Distributions (95%)	Article 11 (c)	✓	
Proceeds from Disposal of Shares (95%)	Article 11 (d)	✓	
Income of Foreign Permanent Establishments (100%)	Article 11 (e)		✓
Deductible Expenses			
General Principle (Obtaining / Securing Income)	Article 12		✓
Stocks and Work-in-Progress			
Initial Measurement (Direct Cost / Option to Include Indirect Cost)	Article 21 / 29 (2)		✓
Simplifying Valuation (FiFo, Weighted-average)	Article 29 (1)		✓
Subsequent Measurement (Lower of Cost and Market)	Article 29 (4)		✓
Bad Debt Receivables			
Specific Allowance (Permitted)	Article 27		✓
General Allowance (Permitted)	Article 27	✓	
Provisions			
Provisions for Liabilities			
Recognition (Permitted, Legal Obligation)	Article 25 (1)	✓	
Measurement	Article 25 (2)	✓	
Provisions for Contingent Losses (Permitted)	Article 25 (1)	✓	
Provision for Deferred Repair and Maintenance Costs (Prohibited)	Article 25 (1)		✓
Warranty Provision (Permitted)	Article 25 (1)		✓
Pension Payments			
Direct Pension Scheme			
Recognition (Permitted)	Article 25 / 26	✓	
Measurement	Article 26	✓	
Indirect Pension Scheme (Permitted)	Article 12		✓

Selected Issues of the Proposed Council Directive	Article	Deviation from Current Practice in the 27 EU Member States, Switzerland and the US	
		Major	Minor
Other Deductible Items: Depreciation			
General Principles and Depreciation Base			
Entitlement to Depreciation (Economic Owner)	Article 34 / 4 (20)		✓
Timing of Depreciation (Full Year's Depreciation)	Article 37 (1)	✓	
Depreciation Base (Full Cost)	Article 33 (1)		✓
Research Costs (not Capitalised)	Article 12		✓
Development Costs (not Capitalised)	Article 12	✓	
Improvement Costs (Capitalised)	Article 35 / 4 (18)		✓
Regular Depreciation			
Low-value Assets (EUR 1,000; Immediately Expensed)	Article 13 / 4 (14)		✓
Internally Developed Intangibles (Immediately Expensed)	Article 36 (1) (c) / 4 (14)		✓
Individually Depreciable Assets (Buildings, Acquired Intangibles, Machinery and Equipment (Useful Life > 15 years))	Article 33 (1) / 36 (1)		✓
Asset Pool (Machinery and Equipment (Useful Life ≤ 15 years))	Article 39	✓	
Exceptional Depreciation			
Depreciable Assets (Prohibited)	Article 41		✓
Assets not Subject to Depreciation (Permitted)	Article 41	✓	
Non-deductible Expenses			
Group 1: Benefits Granted, Profit Distributions etc.	Article 14 (1) / 15		✓
Group 2: Tax Payments	Article 14 (1)	✓	
Group 3: Fines, Entertainment, Exempt Income	Article 14 (1)		✓
Group 4: Interest Expenses	Article 81	✓	
Losses			
Loss Carryforward (No Restrictions; Neither Amount nor Timing)	Article 43	✓	

Selected Issues of the Proposed Council Directive	Article	Deviation from Current Practice in the 27 EU Member States, Switzerland and the US	
		Major	Minor
Loss Carryback (Prohibited)	Article 43		✓
Loss Trafficking Rules (Not Applicable)	Article 71	✓	
Total: Summary Results		**19**	**33**

Overall, the summary results displayed in Table E-1 reveal that the differences between the proposed Council Directive and international tax accounting practice are of minor importance. Moreover, considering the 52 different elements of the proposed Council Directive that have been analysed in detail, most deviations from prevailing tax practice are of formal or technical nature and are therefore expected to have insignificant impacts on the actual amount of taxable income. However, significant and substantial differences are identified with regard to the recognition and measurement of provisions, depreciation rates and methods, capital gains taxation as well as the tax relief for losses. Considering these results, we are convinced that the CCTB is appropriate to replace the existing determination of corporate taxable income under national tax accounting rules in the Member States. Further quantitative assessment on the impact of a CCTB on the effective tax burdens of corporations and tax revenue respectively is, however, still necessary to finally evaluate the proposal. In addition, some open questions remain that must be addressed in more detail once the proposed Council Directive is to be implemented into the tax law of the Member States.

A Call for Clarity: Some Open Questions (see Section D.2)

Considering the first step of a CCCTB only, i.e. the determination of a CCTB without consolidation and formula apportionment, two categories of open questions raise practical concerns and require – from our perspective – further clarification in the ongoing evaluation process. These concerns can be identified as follows:

(1) Authoritative interpretation and regulations on the application of the proposed Council Directive:

   If the proposed Council Directive should serve as an autonomous set of rules for the determination of a harmonised tax base across Member States, further regulations and authoritative interpretation appear to be necessary. Such regulations must provide comprehensive and detailed guidelines on the interpretation and application of more than 80 Articles of the proposed Council Directive dealing with the determination of a CCTB. In this regard, neither the basic principles nor the definitions provided for the recognition and measurement of revenue and expenses seem to be sufficient enough to guarantee a common and uniform understanding of tax accounting. Moreover, clear legal concepts have to be established for special areas of tax accounting, e.g. leasing arrangements, in order to assure a uniform application of the proposed Council Directive across Member States. Based on our analysis of the national tax accounting practice in the Member States, Switzerland and the US, we presents a non-exhaustive list of concerns about the practical application of the proposed Council Directive that require further consideration in the ongoing evaluation process. (Table 11, Section D.2.3).

(2) Achieving an objective, certain and uniform Common Corporate Tax Base:

Objectivity is a guiding principle of tax policy. In order to achieve a common and uniform application of tax accounting practice across Member States it is crucial to establish a mandatory system. Objective in this sense means that the CCTB is to be implemented without any accounting options for the taxpayer. The regulations dealing with the measurement of stock items lack this objectivity: Both the option to base the initial measurement on direct or indirect costs and the choice to apply either the FiFo or the weighted average cost method are inconsistent with a objective and uniform taxation across Member States. In this regard, definite regulations are advisable. Furthermore, open questions remain with respect to the treatment of differences between the proposed Council Directive and national tax accounting on transition to the CCCTB. In particular, we may question how to handle differences that may arise in recognising and valuing provisions, e.g. if the Euribor for obligations with a maturity of 12 months and the discounting rate applied under national corporate tax law differ. Finally, the coexistence of common and national loss relief regulations as governed by Article 48 causes considerable administrative difficulties and jeopardises the idea of a uniform application of the harmonised tax base.

Summary

The main findings are summarised as follows:

(1) On March 16, 2011, the European Commission released a Draft Council Directive providing multinational companies with a Common Consolidated Corporate Tax Base (CCCTB) for their EU-wide activities.
(2) The CCCTB is a proposal to provide companies with the opportunity to determine taxable income at the level of each group member following a three-step approach: (1) Determination of individual income based on a harmonised set of tax accounting regulations, (2) consolidation of individual incomes and (3) allocation of the consolidated tax base by formula apportionment.
(3) As the second and the third step of a CCCTB, i.e. the consolidation and the allocation mechanism, still suffer from considerable shortcomings, we recommend introducing the CCCTB in two steps. The first step comprises the replacement of the national tax accounting regulations across Member States by

a single set of harmonised tax rules. Such Common Corporate Tax Base (CCTB) would merely affect the calculation of the corporate tax base. Consolidation of individual incomes and the allocation of the consolidated tax base would, however, be omitted for the present and considered at a later stage of tax harmonisation in Europe.

(4) Our study contributes to the ongoing evaluation of the proposed Council Directive. For the first time, details on the determination of taxable income under the proposed Council Directive are compared to prevailing corporate tax accounting regulations as of January 1, 2011 in all 27 Member States, Switzerland and the US.

(5) The results of our study reveal that the differences between the regulations for the determination of taxable income under the proposed Council Directive and current international tax practice are of minor importance. Moreover, many deviations from prevailing tax accounting practices are of formal or technical nature and are expected to have insignificant impacts on the actual amount of taxable income.

(6) Significant and substantial differences are identified with regard to capital gains taxation, the recognition and measurement of provisions, depreciation rates and methods as well as the tax relief for losses.

(7) Considering the results of the international comparison, we are convinced that a CCTB as established by the proposed Council Directive is appropriate to replace the existing rules for the determination of corporate taxable income governed by national tax accounting regulations in the Member States.

(8) Further quantitative assessment on the impact of a CCTB on the effective tax burdens of corporations and tax revenue respectively is necessary to finally evaluate the proposal. In addition, some open questions remain that have to be addressed in more detail once the proposed Council Directive is to be implemented into the tax law of the Member States. These open questions mainly cover comprehensive regulations for the interpretation and application of the regulations of the proposed Council Directive governing the determination of taxable income. Moreover, clear legal concepts have to be established for special areas of tax accounting, e.g. leasing arrangements, in order to assure a uniform application of the proposed Council Directive across Member States.

A. Introduction

On March 16, 2011, the European Commission released a Draft Council Directive on a Common Consolidated Corporate Tax Base (CCCTB), accompanied by a broad and detailed impact assessment.[2] The current initiative by the European Commission restarted the long-lasting public debate on harmonising corporate taxation in the European Union (EU), which had already been launched by the Commission in 2001.[3] In short, the proposed CCCTB would imply a three-step approach:

(1) Determination of corporate taxable income of group members based on a harmonised set of tax accounting regulations;
(2) Consolidation of the individual, i.e. the group members', corporate tax bases to the common tax base;
(3) Allocation of the consolidated tax base to group members located in the different Member States by formula apportionment.

Each Member State would still preserve its right to tax the allocated share of the consolidated tax base applying its own national corporate tax rate.

With the proposal for a CCCTB, the European Commission aims to constitute a fundamental change of corporate taxation in Europe in order to reduce existing inefficiencies and distortions resulting from the co-existence of 27 different tax regimes, and to create an integrated single market for doing business in Europe.[4] Major benefits from the introduction of the proposed CCCTB are seen in the elimination of transfer pricing concerns, the removal of double taxation due to conflicting tax claims between Member States and, of course, in the reduction of administrative burdens and tax compliance cost. At the same time, the proposed Council Directive raises a number of new issues. Examples include transitional rules for the entry and exit of group members referring to the taxation of hidden reserves or the treatment of third-country relations.

As the Commission seeks for the proposed Council Directive to be approved by the EU Council in 2013, now is the time for Member States to discuss these issues and assess the economic benefits from corporate tax harmonisation. While not all of the national positions are known to date, some EU Member States have clearly expressed scepticism. In particular, what is found to be missing from the European Commission and, of course, the academic literature is convincing evidence on the

---

[2] The full Council Directive on a Common Consolidated Corporate Tax Base (CCCTB) is available for download under http://ec.europa.eu/taxation_customs/resources/documents/taxation/company_tax/common_tax_base/com_2011_121_en.pdf.

[3] See Commission of the European Communities (2001).

[4] See for a discussion of tax obstacles to cross-border economic activities in the internal market Devereux (2004), pp. 72 ff.

direct economic and revenue impact from introducing a consolidation and sharing mechanism.[5] In this respect, further discussion and consideration, which is not likely to be available within the near future, seems necessary to fully understand and evaluate the consequences of any consolidation and sharing mechanism and convince Member States that the gains from harmonisation are worth the costs of giving up sovereignty in corporate tax policy.

Overall, it is at least questionable whether all or even some Member States (via enhanced cooperation) will adopt the CCCTB system in its current scope.[6] Therefore, the European Commission should also consider a strategy that would introduce the CCCTB in two steps. The first step simply includes the replacement of the 27 national tax accounting regulations across Member States by a single set of harmonised tax rules. Such Common Corporate Tax Base (CCTB) would merely affect the calculation of the corporate tax base. The second and the third step of a CCCTB, i.e. the consolidation of individual group members' income and the subsequent allocation of the consolidated tax base, would be omitted for the present. Although, some of the fundamental advantages of the CCCTB would, of course, not be realised by the introduction of a CCTB, the two-step approach seems more likely to succeed through the political process in the EU and appears to be a promising starting-point for corporate tax harmonisation. In this respect, the promoted convergence of the French and German tax systems, on which the two tax administrations are currently working, could have a substantial impact on other Member States.[7]

Against this background, it is the purpose of this study to contribute to the ongoing evaluation of the concept of a CCCTB. For the first time the rules for the determination of taxable income under the proposed Council Directive are analysed and compared to those in all 27 Member States, Switzerland and the US. The focus of this study is on the first step of a CCTB, i.e. the determination of corporate taxable income at the level of each group member (CCTB). More precisely, we aim to contribute to the question whether a CCTB as established in the proposed Council Directive is appropriate to replace national tax accounting regulations in the Member States. In doing so, Ernst & Young (EY) tax experts in all 29 considered countries have been asked to provide detailed information on the fundamental concepts of tax accounting, the recognition of revenue and expenses and the loss relief under the national tax codes currently in practice. In detail, EY members firms in the respective countries have received and responded to a jointly developed questionnaire that includes more than 80 questions concerning all important matters regulated by the proposed Council Directive. The information provided allow for a detailed and comprehensive comparison of the CCTB and the rules on the determination of corporate taxable income across Member States as of 2011.

---

[5] Please note that Fuest/Hemmelgarn/Ramb (2007), Devereux/Loretz (2008) and Oestreicher/Koch (2011) provide first promising assessments of the change from separate accounting to formula apportionment and the consequences of the implementation of a CCCTB.

[6] See also Fuest (2008), p. 738.

[7] See press conference of German Federal Chancellor Merkel and French President Sarkozy on August 17th, 2011.

The international comparison, however, neither intends to evaluate the tax rules proposed in the Council Directive or in the considered countries nor does it aim to review and discuss all elements and items of the currently implemented tax systems in Europe in full detail. Rather, the main characteristics of the national tax regulations and the most important origins of differences between the proposed CCCTB regulations and the national tax practices are to be identified and analysed. In addition, the study elaborates whether the proposed Council Directive addresses all major elements for the determination of taxable business income. Yet, the study's objective is not only to provide evidence of differences in the determination of taxable income across Europe, but it should also serve as a valuable source for understanding how the proposed CCCTB would affect corporate tax burdens and budget revenues in Europe. In this regard, the first relevant question to answer is to which extent the tax base determined under the rules in the proposed Council Directive will differ from the one determined under current national practice.

The structure of this study is as follows: Section B briefly reviews the current state of the CCCTB project, provides an overview of the proposed Council Directive and discusses some important advantages and open questions raised by the proposal. Section C focuses on the results obtained from comparing the regulations of the proposed Council Directive with current tax practice in the 27 EU Member States, Switzerland and the US. We include Switzerland since it is a core member of Europe. The consideration of the US is based on the fact that consolidated taxation and formula apportionment is applied for state taxation since the early 20th century in the US.[8] Thus, the comparison of the proposed Council Directive with US tax practice seems to be promising and offers opportunities to translate lessons learned from US practice into developments in the European Union. In particular, Section C systematically discusses the individual regulations, compares them in an international setting and identifies elements of taxable income, which are not explicitly addressed by the proposed Council Directive. Subsequently the most important differences between the proposed Council Directive and national tax accounting regulations are summarised in Section D. Moreover, the main areas that are not covered by the proposed Council Directive or that, from our perspective, must be addressed in more detail are identified, discussed and separately presented. Finally, Section E summarises the main results.

---

[8]   See Weiner (2005), pp. 10-15.

B. Common Corporate (Consolidated) Tax Base: Some Institutional Details

The current initiatives of the European Commission are based on the 2001 report "Company Taxation in the Internal Market".[9] The Commission believes that only a comprehensive solution is suitable to eliminate tax obstacles in the EU systematically. The long-term objective in removing tax obstacles to cross-border business activities is the introduction of a CCCTB for the EU-wide activities of multinationals. In short, the proposed CCCTB would imply a three-step approach:

(1) Determination of corporate taxable income of group members based on a harmonised set of tax accounting regulations; (Articles 9 – 43);
(2) Consolidation of the individual, i.e. the group members', corporate tax bases to the common tax base (Articles 54 – 60);
(3) Allocation of the consolidated tax base to group members located in different Member States by formula apportionment (Articles 86 – 103).

The proposed CCCTB would, however, neither interfere with financial accounting regulations nor would it harmonise tax rates. Consequently, each Member State would maintain its national rules on financial accounting and preserve its right to tax the allocated portion of the consolidated tax base at the level of each group member applying its own national corporate tax rate. Tax competition based on national corporate tax rates within the EU is explicitly encouraged by a CCCTB.

The proposed Council Directive applies to so-called eligible EU companies. A eligible company must take one of the forms listed in Annex I to the proposed Council Directive and must be subject to corporate taxation in a Member State as listed in Annex II (Article 2). Yet, it should be noted that the proposed CCCTB would be an optional rather than a mandatory system. Companies would, therefore, have the option to remain fully governed by the national tax system or to be taxed under the proposed CCCTB (Article 6). Consequently, Member States would have to administer two corporate tax systems at the same time. The option to apply the proposed CCCTB would be valid for an initial period of five tax years, which could be extended for successive terms of three tax years, unless notice of termination is given (Article 105). Companies that opt for the proposed CCCTB system would only file a single tax return with the so-called principal tax authority in one Member State (one-stop-shop system) for the group's entire activities in the EU (Article 109). Thus, all communication would take place solely between the principal taxpayer of the group and the tax authority to which it is assigned. Furthermore, when the option to apply the proposed CCCTB is exercised all qualifying subsidiaries are automatically consolidated (the all-in, all-out principle). According to Article 54,

---

[9] See Commission of the European Communities (2001).

qualifying subsidiaries include all immediate and lower-tier subsidiaries, in which the parent company holds a right to exercise more than 50% of the voting rights, an ownership amounting to more than 75% of the company's capital or more than 75% of the rights giving entitlement to profit. In general, the thresholds must be met throughout the year (Article 58).

B.1. The CCCTB: A Shift in Paradigm

The consolidation and allocation of group income to the individual group members represents a paradigm shift in corporate taxation. In order to understand how this paradigm shift is meant to work, it is helpful to consider the limits of separate entity accounting currently in practice and the aimed benefits of consolidation and formula apportionment.

Consolidating the separately determined profits of group members makes it impossible to maintain the prevailing system of direct allocation of profits using transfer prices based on the arm's length principle for individual transactions (separate entity accounting). Instead, consolidating the individual results requires an indirect division of the profits of the consolidated overall result using a formula, i.e. breaking down the group's result among the individual group companies (formula apportionment). Formula apportionment has a long tradition in North America, e.g. group taxation at the level of the States (US) or at the level of the Provinces (Canada).[10] As mentioned above, the rationale for formula apportionment begins with the limits of separate entity accounting. Concerning economically integrated groups of companies, the transactional approach seems theoretically questionable. By setting up an integrated group of companies, coordination of transactions via markets is abandoned in favour of coordination using intra-organisational hierarchies. The aim is to generate economies of integration, for example by means of lower transaction costs, improvement of information flow or managerial efficiency.[11] As a result, the profits of an integrated group of companies are higher than the aggregate profits earned by its separate entities. Since the excess profits accrue at group level, it seems difficult to determine the source of these profits as they cannot be attributed to specific and, above all, individual transactions either. Therefore, the comparison of controlled transactions to uncontrolled transactions – as the arm's length principle implies – seems conceptually questionable and systematically inapplicable.[12] Double taxation constitutes another problem arising in the context of the arm's length principle. One tax jurisdiction may adjust a given transfer price because it is deemed not to be at arm's length. If the other jurisdiction does not agree to a corresponding adjustment, there is a risk of double taxation.[13]

Against this background, the current international tax system is inadequate with reference to the principles of efficiency and neutrality as well as simplicity and enforceability. The arm's length principle ignores the differences between control-

---

[10]   See Weiner (2005), pp. 10-15; Mintz/Weiner (2003), pp. 695-711.
[11]   See Berry/Bradford/Hines (1992), p. 737.
[12]   See McLure (1984), pp. 94, 105; Jacobs/Endres/Spengel (2011), p. 661.
[13]   See Newlon (2000), pp. 220-221.

led and uncontrolled transactions and entails the scope for abusive transfer pric-ing.[14] It is incapable of fairly allocating profits to the countries involved according to their source and, thus inconsistent with the principle of internation equity.[15] At the same time, double taxation, which arises if transfer prices are adjusted unilater-ally, violates the principle of equity between taxpayers.[16]

Under the proposed CCCTB, the arm's length principle as a means for the allo-cation of taxable income between jurisdictions would be replaced by formula apportionment. Formula apportionment does not seek to allocate income to its source perfectly. Rather, the rationale behind formula apportionment is to provide a pragmatic solution for profit allocation among jurisdictions in order to better cope with the issues of simplicity and enforceability. Yet, formula apportionment is not arbitrary. Depending on the choice of apportionment factors, this approach intends to allocate the consolidated tax base to the profit generating activities. Factors which are deemed to represent profit generating activities under the proposed CCCTB are sales, payroll, number of employees and the assets of the company. Considering a company, A, which belongs to a group of companies being taxed under the proposed CCCTB, the apportionment formula thus reads as follows (Article 86):

$$Share_A = \left[\frac{1}{3} \times \frac{Sales_A}{Sales_{Group}} + \frac{1}{3} \times \left(\frac{1}{2} \times \frac{Payroll_A}{Payroll_{Group}} + \frac{1}{2} \times \frac{Employees_A}{Employees_{Group}}\right) + \frac{1}{3} \times \frac{Asssets_A}{Assets_{Group}}\right] \times CTB$$

with CTB representing the consolidated overall result of the group.[17]

At this point, it may be helpful to consider a simplified example in order to understand the tax implications of the sharing mechanism. Consider a group that consists of company A and company B. Company A resides and sells its output in Member State X and company B resides and sell its output in Member States Y. Required information regarding sales, payroll, employees and assets for both com-panies are provided in Table 1.

---

[14] See Avi-Yonah/Benshalom (2011).
[15] See Jacobs/Spengel/Schäfer (2004), pp. 272-273.
[16] See Li (2002), p. 840.
[17] For the composition and other details on the sales, labour and asset factor see Article 90-97 of the proposed Council Directive. For another example of the application of formula apportion-ment, see Fuest (2008), pp. 724-725.

Table 1: Example for the Application of Formula Apportionment

Country		Member State X	Member State Y
Company A	Sales	40	
	Payroll and Employees	40	
	Assets	40	
	Taxable Income	30	
Company B	Sales		80
	Payroll and Employees		20
	Assets		20
	Taxable Income		60
Tax Rate		10%	30%

Considering the given information above, the tax burden under separate accounting per company and the total tax burden for the group amounts to 21:

$$T_A = 30 \times 0.1 = 3; \quad T_B = 60 \times 0.3 = 18; \quad T_A + T_B = 3 + 18 = \mathbf{21}$$

Applying the apportionment formula according to Article 86 and assuming an identical tax base, the tax burden per company and the total tax burden for the group amounts to 17:

$$T_A = 0.1 \times (30 + 60) \times \left(\frac{1}{3} \times \frac{40}{120} + \frac{1}{3} \times \frac{40}{60} + \frac{1}{3} \times \frac{40}{60} \right) = 5$$

$$T_B = 0.3 \times (30 + 60) \times \left(\frac{1}{3} \times \frac{80}{120} + \frac{1}{3} \times \frac{20}{60} + \frac{1}{3} \times \frac{20}{60} \right) = 12$$

$$T_A + T_B = 5 + 12 = \mathbf{17}$$

The simple example illustrates that formula apportionment would significantly change the total tax burden for groups of companies and may provide incentives to increase EU-wide tax rate competition. Obviously, the tax implications depend on the relation of the apportionment factors and on the tax rates stipulated by the Member States.

As the Commission recognises that applying the general formula may lead to unfair or inappropriate results, Article 87 provides a safeguard clause allowing the taxpayer or the authority concerned to request the use of an alternative method. Furthermore, Articles 98 – 101 provide variations of the general formula for specific sectors, e.g. financial institutions, transport or insurance undertakings.

B.2. Advantages: Overcoming Tax Obstacles to Cross-Border Activities

The main objective stressed in the proposed Council Directive is to tackle major fiscal impediments to growth in the Single Market that are caused by the interaction of 27 different national tax systems. The proposed CCCTB is expected to con-

tribute to the elimination of tax obstacles to cross-border EU-wide activities in several ways. Namely, the CCCTB is to solve the problem of double-taxation as a
result of conflicting taxing rights, reduce compliance and administrative costs and
remove distortions caused by limitations of cross-border loss relief and reorganisations within the EU. Table 2 summarises some of the major objectives and illustrates whether the proposed CCCTB is capable to overcome the existing obstacles
to cross-border activities in the EU. As the Commission should also consider a
strategy that would introduce the CCCTB in two steps if there is no unanimous
support among the Member States, Table 2 also lists the achievements realised
under a CCTB.[18]

Table 2: Reduction / Elimination of Tax Obstacles to Cross-Border EU-Wide Activities
by the CC(C)TB

Reduction / Elimination of Tax Obstacles to Cross-border Activities	Approaches with Different Degree of International Cooperation	
	Common Corporate Tax Base throughout the EU (CCTB)	**Common Corporate Consolidated Tax Base throughout the EU (CCCTB)**
Compliance Costs	Achieved	Achieved
Cross-border Loss Relief	Not achieved, but simplified Except to the extent that Member States already provide cross-border loss relief	Achieved
Transfer Prices	Not achieved, but simplified Transfer prices are still required for the allocation of the tax base	Achieved Transfer prices are substituted by formula apportionment
Reorganisations	Not achieved, but simplified Only if the tax treatment of reorganisations is harmonised	Achieved Only if the tax treatment of reorganisations is harmonised
Double Taxation as a Result of Conflicting Taxation Rights	Not achieved	Achieved

As displayed in Table 2, the proposed CCCTB has to be established in order to
fully eliminate tax obstacles to cross-border activities within the EU. First, with the
introduction of the proposed CCCTB many forms of profit shifting through transfer
pricing disappear among companies participating in the CCCTB. Further benefits
lie in consolidating taxable profits: The consolidation of the individual results of
the group members yields cross-border loss compensation at the level of the taxable entity. Furthermore, supplies and services may generally be invoiced at the
respective tax book value as only profits realised from transactions with third parties are distributed among the group companies by the allocation of profits. This

---

[18]   For the following, see also Spengel (2008), Spengel/Wendt (2008) and Spengel/Malke (2009).

eliminates inter-company profits taking the single economic unit argument into account. Moreover, the group's tax burden cannot be influenced by changing intra-group financing, so that measures to limit shareholder debt financing (thin-capitalisation rules) and CFC regulations – at least within countries participating in the CCCTB – would become obsolete.[19] Furthermore, costs for refinancing are deducted from the consolidated group income and apportioned to all Member States in which group members are resident rather than from individual income. Finally, hidden reserves upon cross-border reorganisations or the transfer of assets do not have to be taxed immediately; they are divided among the group members according to the allocation formula upon realisation, irrespective of where the profits are generated. Formula apportionment thus abolishes the incentives to transfer book profits from one group member to another. To this extent, the proposed CCCTB takes away most of the companies' tax-planning opportunities but, on the other hand, abolishes obstacles to cross-border business activities, reduces Member States' conflicts with EU-law and increases the Member States' tax autonomy.

In the case of a CCTB, merely a harmonised set of tax accounting regulations for the determination of corporate taxable income would be applied across Member States. Even though a CCTB would obviously give rise to new challenges for both, tax authorities and companies[20], the CCTB is likely to reduce compliance and administrative costs.[21] In contrast, all other tax obstacles on cross-border activities identified above would generally remain. A closer look, however, reveals several important advancements: First, a CCTB is a prerequisite for any form of cross-border loss relief within the EU. Without harmonisation of the tax base, separate accounting rules for the determination of foreign losses – with all the attendant difficulties associated with the recapture of loss relief if the foreign subsidiary claims its own relief later – have to be maintained. Second, although transfer pricing would obviously remain an issue under a CCTB system, both tax authorities and companies would benefit from harmonised tax accounting regulations in several ways. Most obviously, given that transfer prices are usually calculated in accordance with (tax) accounting principles for the purpose of applying cost-based methods (e.g. the cost plus method), difficulties associated with determining the cost base for cross-border transactions in the same manner would become much more manageable. Finally, a harmonised corporate tax base clearly facilitates cross-border reorganisation and international cooperation between Member States. As assets and liabilities would be recognised and measured under the identical set of regulations in all Member States, adopting a system of a CCTB would reduce many of the uncertainties, administrative burdens and threats of double taxation in cross-border reorganisations.

---

[19] Please note that the proposed Council Directive provide both CFC-Rules (Article 82 and 83) as well as thin-capitalisation rules (Article 81). Yet, it should be noted that the regulations laid down in Articles 81 to 83 are more or less relevant only to associated enterprises resident in a third-country.

[20] Most important, tax authorities will have to administer two corporate tax systems instead of one if the CC(C)TB – as proposed by the Commission – is optional.

[21] See also Schreiber (2009), p. 91.

To conclude, while only the proposed CCCTB would eliminate or at least reduce major tax obstacles to cross-border activities in the EU, the introduction of a mere CCTB, i.e. a CCCTB without consolidation and formula apportionment, would also offer benefits to both tax authorities and companies. As it avoids many of the technical challenges and difficult issues raised by the proposed CCCTB - some of which will be discussed below - the CCTB appears to be a promising starting-point for corporate tax harmonisation in the EU.

B.3. Implementation Issues: Some Critical Comments

As already mentioned above, the proposed Council Directive raises a number of difficulties, new issues and technical challenges. Important examples include the entry and exit rules referring to the taxation of hidden reserves or questions regarding a minimum corporate tax rate. Hence, in this subchapter, we discuss some issues and obstacles on the way to the proposed CCCTB, including some general issues, e.g. the administration of the CCCTB or the treatment of third country in- and outbound investment, questions arising in the context of tax planning and issues of transition, i.e. the entry to and the exit from the proposed CCCTB. All issues discussed reveal more or less unsolved problems arising from introducing a consolidation and sharing mechanism and make a good case for the European Commission to consider the strategy of introducing the CCCTB in a two-step approach. Again, the first step would introduce a harmonised set of tax accounting rules at the level of each company. These tax accounting rules could be applied to group members as well as to individual companies. Under a CCCTB there is no obvious reason why it should be denied to individual companies. The second step then would introduce consolidation and formula apportionment at a later stage.

Formula Apportionment: Some General Issues

a.) Factors in the Formula: Intangibles

As noted above, factors which are deemed to represent profit generating activities under the proposed CCCTB are sales, payroll, the number of employees and the fixed assets of the company. In contrast, intangible assets are excluded from the asset factor under the current scope of the proposal (Article 92). Yet, intangible assets constitute an important part of the total asset and the economic presence of multinationals.[22] In this regard, a key issue that arises is whether the exclusion of intangibles yields inappropriate and unfair results as unduly low shares of the common tax base would be allocated to those group members developing intangibles.[23] Obviously, the European Commission has considered this issue but faces a trade-off: On the one hand, intangible assets clearly constitute a substantial factor in the value chain and, therefore, should be included in the measures of assets. On the other hand, it is inherently difficult to measure

---

[22] See McLure/Weiner (2000), p. 269.
[23] For a detailed discussion on formula apportionment and the role of intangible assets, see Avi-Yonah/Benshalom (2011).

the value of intangibles.[24] Furthermore, due to their mobile nature intangibles provide ample room for manipulation of the sharing mechanism. Although the exclusion provided for in Article 92 (1) thus seems attractive from a pragmatic and administrative point of view, there are also good reasons to take the key value represented by intangibles for companies into account. It remains to be discussed if the adjustment of the asset factor provided for in Article 92 (2), stating that the costs incurred for R&D, marketing and advertising in the six years prior to a company entering the CCCTB would be included as a proxy for intangible assets for five years, represents a way out of this trade-off and prohibits unfair and unequal apportionment.

b.) Tax Administration: One-Stop-Shop

Since no European tax administration has been established at the current stage of development of the European Union, the proposed CCCTB must be governed by national tax authorities. In doing so, the proposed Council Directive provides for a so-called one-stop-shop system (Article 104 – 126), under which a single Member State (principal tax authority) is responsible for administrating all tax affairs of a given group represented by its principal taxpayer. While the proposed one-stop-shop system is clearly necessary in order to reduce compliance costs of dealing with up to 27 national tax authorities, its administrative and procedural framework raises several concerns beyond mere incentive problems.[25] Most important, the fact that one national tax authority would be responsible for the entire group requires considerable cooperation and coordination between national tax authorities in a form yet unknown within the EU. This cooperation includes the exchange of information, close consultation and the support of smaller countries in administrating and monitoring large multinational groups if they lack the capacity. How all of this would work in practice is to date somewhat unclear. The same holds true for audits and the management of disagreements between Member States. Despite the regulation laid down in Article 122 and Article 123, more precise common standards have to be found in this respect in order to ensure a coordinated, correct and fair tax administration within the EU.[26]

Finally, clarification is needed concerning the authoritative interpretation of the regulations of the proposed Council Directive. Leaving interpretation decisions to national courts may yield non-uniform taxation and a common tax base that is harmonised only on paper, but not in practice. In this respect, the crucial point is the implementation of a supreme court allowing authoritative interpretation of the Directive from a central body, e.g. a European Tax Court or special chambers at the European Court of Justice. Notably, under this approach national courts would be obligated to refer to the central body in any case of doubt.

---

[24] See Sørensen (2004), p. 97.
[25] For details, see subchapter C.3.2 and Fuest (2008), p. 738.
[26] See for details Cerioni (2011), pp. 527-529.

c.) **Third Countries: Treatment of Outbound and Inbound Investments**

The territorial scope of the proposed CCCTB is, in general terms, limited to the boundaries of the EU; however, consideration has also to be given to business activities between Member States and third countries. In this respect, outbound and inbound investment can be distinguished. Regarding outbound investment, the proposed Council Directive principally provides clear guidance on how foreign source income is taxed: Dividends received (Article 11 (c)) and income from permanent establishments (Article 11 (e)) in third countries are generally tax exempt. Indeed, certain anti-abuse rules, e.g. CFC regulations (Article 82) or switch-over regulations for tax exempt income (Article 73), apply if a minimum tax rate is undercut. Yet, to the extent that such foreign-income will be taxed, questions arise regarding the sharing of this taxable income among the members of the group and the determination of the tax credit.[27] Whether the regulations provided by Article 76 are adequate to limit tax planning and avoid double taxation is an open issue that clearly needs further consideration. The same holds true for the taxation of inbound investment. In this regard, an unsolved problem arises mainly due to the fact that different companies within the same group would be affected by a number of different national rules and tax treaties. As the proposed Council Directive does not include a harmonisation of aspects of international taxation with respect to transactions outside the territorial scope of the proposed CCCTB,[28] different rules apply for cross-border investment between group members and non-EU group entities facilitating strategic tax planning. As a result, EU companies might reorganise their businesses within the EU in a way that cross-border investments in third countries are subject to the most beneficial rules provided by a Member State.[29]

Overall, the lack of harmonisation of cross-border regulations gives rise to a number of unresolved problems and demands further examination and a clear understanding of how to coordinate international aspects of taxation and tax treaties in order to make the proposed CCCTB functional. At least in the long run, common rules for taxing income with respect to third countries are recommended.[30] In this respect, a common starting point may be the respective regulations of the OECD Model Treaty.

Formula Apportionment and Tax Planning: In Favour of a Minimum Tax Rate

The CCCTB and formula apportionment as proposed by the European Commission is not guarded against strategic tax planning. There is leeway for profit shifting, as the apportionment factors (sales, payroll, number of employees and the assets of the company) are mobile across jurisdictions. Obviously, there might be an incentive for companies to reallocate economic activities that comprise the apportion-

---

[27] See for details Fuest (2008), p. 736.
[28] See also Devereux/Loretz (2011), p. 7; Spengel/Wendt (2008).
[29] For details see Spengel (2008), pp. 39-40.
[30] See also Hellerstein/McLure (2004) p. 207; Mintz (2004), p. 228.

ment factors to low tax jurisdictions in order to reduce the effective tax rate.[31] For instance, if the investment in low tax jurisdictions considerably reduces the effective tax rate applied to the consolidated tax base, investments in companies which are resident in low tax jurisdictions may be carried out even if these companies are not profitable.

By reallocating business functions entering the allocation formula, multinationals are able to shift a greater portion of the tax base to other Member States compared to the prevailing division of the tax base applying transfer prices. Such a reallocation is promoted by the proposed CCCTB as the transfer of functions does not constitute a taxable event due to the elimination of inter-company profits. Given the considerable EU-wide range of nominal tax rates,[32] tax competition within the EU will most likely increase.

Increasing tax competition under the proposed CCCTB may provoke Member States to further reduce tax rates on corporate profits. Moreover, it foils the proper functioning of the Common Market if decisions where to locate investments are mainly tax driven. This inevitably raises the question whether the European Commission should rethink its current position in favour of tax competition based on national corporate tax rates and combine the proposed CCCTB with a minimum tax rate on corporate profits. A minimum corporate tax rate has two objectives: First, it protects an efficient allocation of resources and, thus, the economic goals of the Treaty on the Functioning of the European Union. Second, it protects the autonomy of Member States with respect to the personal income tax. Therefore, a harmonised tax base combined with a minimum corporate tax rate serves as a compromise between economic efficiency in the EU and the tax autonomy of Member States.[33]

Entry to and Exit from the CCCTB: Taxation of Hidden Reserves

Entry and exist rules address transitional issues and refer to the taxation of hidden reserves – i.e. differences between market value and tax book value of an asset – in the event that companies are joining or leaving the system.[34] Article 44 of the proposed Council Directive provides that all assets and liabilities are to be recognised at their value as calculated according to the national tax rules, i.e. the tax book value. Taxation is thus deferred until the group realises the transferred hidden reserves. Unrealised capital gains built up in the Member States before entering the system are hence treated under the general rules provided in the proposed Council Directive and are shared according to the allocation mechanism. Yet, hidden reserves built before a company joins the group do not belong to the group. Instead, they belong to the individual company and, therefore, to the respective tax jurisdiction which would lose significant amounts of tax revenues if its taxing right for hidden reserves built up before entering the system would not be secured. Conse-

---

[31] See Weiner (2005), pp. 38-50; Argúndez-Garzía (2006), pp. 59-69.
[32] See Spengel/Zinn (2011), p. 496.
[33] See Sørensen (2004) and Spengel (2007), p. 120.
[34] For a detailed discussion on the different obstacles surrounding the entry to and the exit from the CCCTB, see also Schreiber (2009) and Spengel (2008), pp. 40-41.

quently, detailed rules are required, in particular for self-created intangible assets that are, in general, not capitalised, in order to take proper account of Member State's taxing rights. Whether the proposed grandfathering rules of Article 61 are sufficient enough to secure Member State's taxing rights and avoid unbalanced outcomes is - in particular against the background of tax planning potential – at least questionable. According to Article 61 the proceeds of the disposal of non-depreciable or individually depreciable fixed assets should not be included in the consolidated tax base but shall be added to the respective group member's allocated profit share in case the transferred assets are disposed of within five years. In this respect, especially the omission of self-created intangibles from the adjustments to the general sharing mechanism under Article 61 has to be reconsidered. Since self-created intangible assets may be transferred tax free and without any grandfathering regulations under the CCCTB system in its current scope, companies would have enhanced opportunities to make use of tax rate differentials within the EU. In other words, companies may at least to some degree choose where to pay taxes on hidden reserves.[35] Moreover, given the opportunity to move existing assets without tax consequence at tax book values and considering that shareholdings may be disposed of without triggering any tax payments, the proposed Council Directive offers extensive possibilities for artificial tax planning. Again, whether the proposed regulations of Article 68 or Article 75, which prohibit the tax-free disposal of shares if assets are transferred to a company leaving the group within two tax years, are able to avoid such artificial tax planning techniques remains questionable. From the perspective of tax authorities, it is also worth mentioning that any form of grandfathering regulations is not easy to administer. In the contrary, Member States are forced to record, value and monitor all assets that were transferred. This does not only require close cooperation among national tax authorities, but tax administrators in the EU would also still have to maintain separate entity accounts, which significantly reduces the administrative advantages of the proposed CCCTB.[36]

---

[35] See Schreiber (2009), pp. 85 ff.
[36] See Hohenwarter (2008), p. 185.

C. The Determination of Taxable Income: A Comparison of the CCCTB Proposal and Current Practice in the EU Member States, Switzerland and the United States

C.1. Methodology and Scope of the Survey

The comparison of national tax regimes is a challenging task as taxes on corporate income and accounting standards are complex and subject to frequent changes. Available tax databases usually cover just some of the main features of the tax system like statutory rates or general elements of the tax base (e.g. depreciation rules, treatment of losses etc.). Regulations on the fundamental concepts and principles underlying the determination of taxable income are, however, scarcely documented or only available in the language of the countries concerned. Overall, there is only little work available specifically addressing cross-country differences in the determination of corporate taxable income. A similar study is, however, conducted by Endres/Oestreicher/Scheffler/Spengel (2007) providing valuable information on differences between IAS/IFRS and national tax regulations in 25 EU Member States as of the fiscal year 2006.[37] We use this study as guidance when exploring the major differences between the proposed Council Directive and the national tax regulations. In doing so, we not only extend the scope of existing literature by providing up to date information on the proposed Council Directive and tax accounting in Europe (fiscal year 2011), but also enlarge the geographical spectrum of other studies. Besides tax accounting regulations in all 27 EU Member States, we especially take the determination of corporate taxable income in Switzerland and the US into account. Obviously, while Switzerland plays an important role in Europe's economy and tax policy, formula apportionment has – as already mentioned – a long tradition in the US. Therefore, lessons learned from the comparison between the proposed Council Directive and US taxation might be of great value for the evaluation of the economic consequences of the proposed CCCTB.

In order to obtain detailed information and avoid uncertainties with respect to the interpretation of the national tax systems in all 27 EU Member States, Switzerland and the US, we have collected all necessary tax data from Ernst & Young (EY) accountants and tax experts in all 29 considered countries. In detail, we asked the EY country offices to fill out prefilled tax surveys which include more than 80 questions concerning all matters regulated by the proposed Council Directive with respect to the determination of taxable income under the CCCTB. In accord-

---

[37] In addition, Kahle/Schulz (2011b) compare tax accounting regulations in France, Poland and the United Kingdom with IAS/IFRS. Furthermore, Panayi (2011) compares selected elements of the proposed Council Directive with the tax system of the United Kingdom.

ance with the purpose of the study, all sections of the proposal solely dealing with the entry and exit from the CCCTB system (Articles 44 to 53 and 61 to 69), the consolidation (Articles 54 to 60) and the apportionment of the consolidated tax base (Articles 86 to 103) have been omitted from the questionnaire. Furthermore, since the implementation of a mere CCTB would more or less only concern national tax authorities, administrative issues (Article 104 to 126) are not discussed. However, one should bear in mind that the European Court of Justice would play an important role in interpreting elements of the tax base if a CCTB would be adopted.

Please note that all questions asked refer to the regular determination of taxable income of incorporated companies under the national tax regimes as of January 1, 2011. Therefore, the taxation of groups or partnerships, special or simplified rules for SMEs, exceptional rules as well as special incentives (regional, sectional etc.) have been disregarded. Yet, no attention is paid to other more general features of the national tax regulations, such as corporate income tax rates or the taxation of shareholders as this is done in a range of other papers and studies.[38]

The received survey data were double-checked with various publications and information provided by the International Bureau for Fiscal Documentations (IBFD).[39] Discrepancies have been addressed through a second, country-specific questionnaire and further discussion with EY country offices.

The following procedure of describing and evaluating the responses received will be kept throughout the complete analysis: In a first step, emphasis is placed on the proposed rules of the Council Directive. The individual regulations are reviewed and placed in the overall context of determining the tax base under a CCCTB regime. In a second step, the focus will be on the national tax accounting regulations in each of the 27 EU Member States, Switzerland and the US. The international comparison is, as mentioned earlier, not intended to describe all items in full detail. Rather, the main characteristics of the national tax regulations and the most important origins of differences between the proposed CCCTB regulations and the national tax practices are identified and analysed.

C.2. Fundamental Concepts and General Principles

As a starting point, the following subchapter presents and discusses the fundamental concepts underlying the determination of corporate taxable income under the proposed CCCTB and the national tax regulations in the considered countries. Yet, before going into detail on how the tax base is determined, two important points should be made clear: First, the proposed CCCTB system would introduce autonomous rules for computing and determining the tax base of companies and would not interfere with financial accounts. While the debate in preliminary stages has focused on the questions whether and to what extent accounting principles as

---

[38] For an overview of these general features of the national tax regulations, see Spengel/Zinn (2011), pp. 494 ff., and http://ec.europa.eu/taxation_customs/resources/documents/common/publications/studies/etr_company_tax.pdf.

[39] www.ibfd.org.

reflected in the IFRS/IAS could be relied upon,[40] the proposed Council Directive cuts off the formal link between financial and tax accounting. Of course, reviewing the individual regulations similarities to IAS/IFRS are readily identifiable; however, it is important to note that the Council Directive does not provide a formal link or a reference either to national tax accounting principles (GAAP) or to IAS/IFRS. Second, as a formal starting point is missing, it is essential that the proposed Council Directive provides a comprehensive set of general principles and rules that will cover all aspects of determining the common tax base in order to ensure uniform application and treatment across all Member States. Interpretation by reference to national GAAP or national tax rules in matters where uniform treatment is not regulated in the proposed Council Directive – as one may infer from Article 7 – is undesirable and jeopardises the overall objectives of the CCCTB project.[41]

C.2.1. Determination of the Tax Base: Starting Point

As described above, the CCCTB system would introduce autonomous rules for computing and determining the tax base of companies. Although the general principles, e.g. the accrual principle, underlying the proposed CCCTB reflect common accounting principles and practice, the lack of a formal link with IAS/IFRS or national GAAP constitutes one of the most fundamental difference between the proposed Council Directive and the prevailing national rules on tax accounting, which more or less all refer to financial accounts as the starting point for the computation of taxable profits and losses.

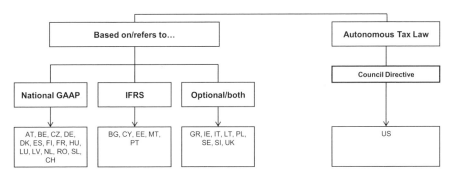

Figure 1: Determination of Taxable Income: Starting Point

Figure 1 shows the nature of the relationship between financial and tax accounting in all 29 considered countries. We find no single country in the European Union where there is no relation between financial accounting and tax accounting. While the degree of dependency of financial accounting for tax accounting obviously differs, there is no doubt that, in all countries considered, the tax base cannot be quantified without the financial accounts as the primary source of information for the tax accounts and a key element in determining the tax base. As a consequence, the

---

[40] See, among others, Spengel (2003), pp. 253 ff. and Schön (2004), pp. 426 ff.
[41] See Spengel/Malke (2008), p. 88 and Freedman/Macdonald (2008).

accrual basis of accounting – recognising transactions and events when they occur and not when cash is received – is central to all considered tax systems as well.[42] Thus, and since financial accounting converges more and more across Europe, differences between the national tax systems cannot be found in the starting point of determining taxable income, but rather in the number and extent of prescribed deviations between financial and tax accounting.

   In detail, 28 of the 29 considered national tax legislations are based or at least rely on the annual income shown in financial accounts, which are subsequently adjusted by specific tax regulations (non-deductible expenses, exemption of specific revenues etc.) in order to determine taxable income. Only the US stipulates a strict separation of tax accountants and commercial accounts.[43] In doing so, the majority of Member States as well as Switzerland do not allow the application of IAS/IFRS as a starting point but rather determine taxable income on the basis of accounts drawn in accordance with national GAAP.[44] Only in Bulgaria, Cyprus, Estonia, Malta and Portugal, the profits shown in the financial accounts drawn up in accordance with IAS/IFRS form, in practice, the basis on which taxable income is determined. In addition, in 8 other countries the accounting treatment under IAS/IFRS may be relevant for corporate income tax purposes for those corporations having adopted IAS/IFRS for financial accounting (e.g. Ireland and Italy). Here, IAS/IFRS may optionally be applied as a starting point for tax accounting.

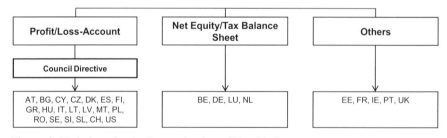

Figure 2: Technique for the Determination of Taxable Income

Thus, what is measured as the tax base in most countries is, in general, determined by accounting principles. The result of the financial accounts is subsequently adjusted by specific tax regulations (non-deductible expenses, exemption of specific revenues, measurement of assets and liabilities etc.). The standard output of the accounting process is either a balance sheet and / or a profit and loss account. It is important to note that both approaches provide the same income if any changes

---

[42] For details, see subchapter C.3.1.1.

[43] Taxable income in the US, however, should be computed under the method of accounting on the basis of which the taxpayer regularly computes his income in keeping his books (Sec. 446 (a) Internal Revenue Code); for details, see Schön (2004), pp. 426 ff.

[44] Yet, as national GAAPs and IAS/IFRS have converged to a considerable extent during the last decade, differences between the national tax systems cannot be found in the starting point of determining taxable income, but rather in the number and extent of prescribed deviations between financial and tax accounting.

in the measurement of assets and liabilities are included in the profit and loss account. Figure 2 shows that under the current national tax systems the profit and loss method is, however, preferred over the tax balance sheet approach. In detail, 20 of the 29 considered countries are in line with the proposed Council Directive computing taxable income based on the result of the profit and loss account. In addition, Ireland and the UK who apply a schedular income tax system that disaggregates income into components and then separately applies tax rates, taxes and exemptions, follow the profit and loss approach for Trading Income. In contrast, Belgium, Germany, Luxembourg and the Netherlands require the comparison of the opening and closing balance sheet and, therefore, a separate tax balance sheet has to be prepared in order to determine corporate taxable income. The regulations in France fall between the two opposite positions as the determination of taxable income can be determined by two different methods, namely the net profit approach or the difference between the net worth at the end and the beginning of the accounting period (balance sheet approach). In Portugal, taxable income is defined as the net income for the period plus certain changes in equity during the same period.

Finally, it has to be pointed out that corporations in Estonia are subject only to a flat-rate tax on distributed profits including transactions that are considered hidden profit distribution. Many issues surrounding the determination of taxable income – as known in all other considered countries – are, therefore, not applicable to the Estonian tax system. Accordingly, attention is paid to Estonia in the following subchapters only where appropriate.

C.2.2. Basic Principles Underlying the Determination of the Tax Base

Besides the realisation principle (Article 9 (1)), which will be discussed in detail in subchapter C.3.1.1., Article 9 of the proposed Council Directive defines two of the general principles underlying the determination of the tax base: First, the item-by-item principal (Article 9 (2)), which states that all transactions and taxable events shall be measured individually, and, second, the consistency requirement (Article 9 (3)), stating that the determination of the tax base shall be carried out in a consistent manner. Additionally, Article 9 (4) provides that the tax base shall be determined for each tax year, which is any twelve-month period, unless otherwise provided by the proposed Council Directive. Apart from these basic principles, Article 80 provides for a general anti-abuse clause. Accordingly, transactions carried out for the sole purpose of avoiding taxation are to be ignored for the purpose of calculating the tax base.

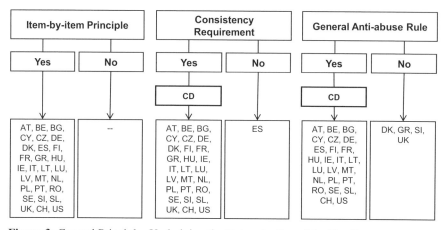

Figure 3: General Principles Underlying the Determination of the Tax Base

Figure 3 summarises the application of these basic principles in each of the considered countries. In general, the basic principles applying to the determination of the tax base under the proposed Council Directive are also valid within the EU, Switzerland and the US. In detail, in all considered countries taxable income is generally determined for a time period of twelve months unless the financial accounting period is shorter (e.g. start-up or cessation periods). Furthermore, the item-by-item principle is followed in all Member States, Switzerland and the US. The same holds true for the consistency requirement, which is relevant in all considered countries except Spain, where consistency is only required in certain cases, e.g. for the depreciation of assets. Differences arise, however, with respect to the implementation of an anti-abuse regulation. While 24 of the considered countries are in line with the proposed Council Directive and provide a general anti-abuse regulation, Denmark, Greece, Slovenia and the United Kingdom[45] have not implemented such regulations in their national tax systems. In addition, it has to be pointed out that the degree of detail of the anti-abuse regulations differs widely across the considered countries. While some countries provide a simple substance-over-form provision (e.g. the Czech Republic or Finland), other countries' tax law includes in-depth anti-avoidance regulations (e.g. Cyprus or Portugal).

Overall, the basic principles applying to the determination of the tax base under the proposed Council Directive are in line with international tax practice and generally suit their purpose. Nevertheless, as neither detailed rules nor authoritative interpretation is yet provided by the Commission, the application of these general principles might cause considerable difficulties and non-uniform treatment in the Member States. A comprehensive framework for the interpretation and application

---

[45] Please note, however, that specific anti-avoidance rules (e.g. thin-capitalisation rules, transfer pricing regulations) exist in Greece, Slovenia and in the United Kingdom. Furthermore, a general anti-avoidance rule might have been developed by the courts or by case law.

of the single regulations still has to be found in order to ensure a common understanding and an unobstructed functionality of the proposed CCCTB.

C.3. Elements of the Tax Base

The determination of the items that are included in the tax base is the central question of all corporate income tax systems.[46] Figure 4 displays the basic concept and elements of the tax base under the proposed CCCTB. The tax base is to be calculated as revenues less exempt revenues, deductible expenses and other deductible items. Accordingly, profit is defined as the excess of revenues over deductible expenses and other deductible items in a tax year (Article 4 (9)) and loss is defined as the excess of deductible expenses and other deductible items over revenue in a tax year (Article 4 (10)). In the following subchapters, each element of the tax base is analysed in more detail.

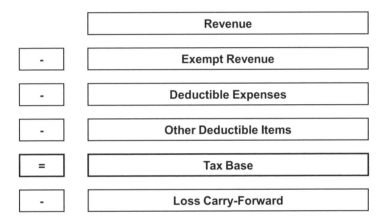

Figure 4: Overview of the Elements of the Tax Base

C.3.1. Revenue

The proposed Council Directive explicitly lists the individual components of revenue in Article 4 (8). All revenues are taxable unless explicitly exempt (Article 10 and 11). In keeping with the profit and loss account based approach, revenue generally is recognised on a transaction basis. Thus, proceeds of both monetary and non-monetary nature are considered to constitute revenue for the purpose of determining the common tax base, including in particular:

(1) Proceeds from sales and other transactions, including proceeds from the disposal of assets and rights, net of value added tax and other taxes and duties;
(2) Interest, dividends and other types of distribution of profits as well as royalties;
(3) Proceeds from liquidation;

---

[46] See Ault/Arnold (2010), p. 199.

(4) Subsidies and grants;

(5) Gifts received, compensation for damages and ex gratia payments; and

(6) Non-monetary gifts made by a taxpayer without consideration.

In contrast, equity raised by the taxpayer and repayments of debt do not constitute revenue.

As all these types of income realised by a company are generally deemed to be taxable income in most countries under consideration, major differences between the national tax systems and the proposed Council Directive cannot be found in individual components, but rather in the timing of revenue. Nonetheless, differences arise with respect to subsidies and grants, which may constitute taxable income in numerous countries under consideration, and the treatment of capital gains. While the latter are computed and taxed separately from revenue in several countries under consideration (e.g. Cyprus or Ireland), proceeds from the disposal of assets and rights are included in ordinary income under the proposed Council Directive if they are not exempt (e.g. proceeds from the disposal of shares).[47]

With regard to the timing of revenue, the international tax accounting practice is, in principal, in line with the realisation principle provided for in Article 9 (1). Almost all countries under consideration recognise revenue only upon realisation. Nevertheless, the interpretation and implementation of the realisation principle takes several forms. Most important, differences can be identified with respect to the extent of departures from the realisation principle, i.e. the taxation of unrealised revenues or the recognition of losses before realisation.[48] In this respect, the proposed Council Directive provides for three major exceptions from the general realisation principle as governed by Article 9 (1): Financial assets and liabilities held for trading (Article 23), long-term contracts (Article 24) and income of controlled foreign companies (Article 82).

C.3.1.1. Timing of Revenue

The timing of revenue under the proposed Council Directive is mainly governed by Articles 9 (1), 17 and 18. Accordingly, profits and losses are to be recognised only when realised (Article 9 (1)). Article 17 provides that revenues, expenses and all other deductible items are to be recognised in the tax year in which they accrue. Revenues accrue when the right to receive them arises and they can be quantified with reasonable accuracy, regardless of the actual payments (Article 18). Except for special regulations for specific industries or small and medium-sized companies, the recognition of revenue on an accrual basis under the proposed Council Directive corresponds with current international tax accounting practice. Rather than applying cash based accounting, taxable income is, in general terms, computed on an accrual basis in all of the countries under consideration (Figure 5). Hence, the majority of countries more or less follow the GAAP frameworks and financial

---

[47] For details on the treatment of capital gains upon the disposal of shares, see subchapter C.3.2.2.

[48] In this regard, another exception can be seen in the allowance for exceptional depreciation under Article 41. For details, see subchapter C.3.4.7.

accounting practice. Only in Denmark, the Netherlands and the US, general revenue recognition criteria are determined separately by tax law or follow established tax practice, e.g. revenue recognition and the realisation date must be determined in accordance to the principle of "sound business practice" in the Netherlands.

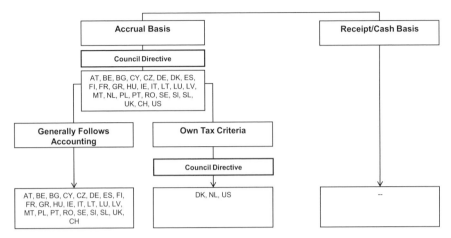

Figure 5: Application of the Accrual Basis of Accounting for Tax Purposes

Moreover, the realisation principle constitutes one of the main tax principles for the purpose of income recognition in all countries under consideration. Yet, as mentioned before, differences arise with respect to the interpretation and implementation of the realisation principle under the proposed Council Directive and tax accounting practice in the countries under consideration. In order to shed light on those differences, the recognition criteria for sales of goods, dividends and interest income are displayed in Figure 6 and discussed in the following.

Revenue from the sale of goods or the provision of services may be recognised by reference to different points of time. Under the proposed Council Directive, sales or service revenues are recognised when the right to receive them arises and the corresponding amount can be quantified with reasonable accuracy, regardless of whether actual payment is deferred (Article 18). Furthermore, as deductible expenses are deemed to be incurred when the significant reward of ownership over the goods has been transferred to the taxpayer (Article 19 (c)), the transfer of significant risks and rewards of ownership is also assumed to be relevant for the purpose of determining the recognition date of sales of goods. The same holds true for most countries under consideration. As displayed in Figure 6, there is, in principle, no significant difference between the proposed Council Directive and international tax practice. While 8 of the 28 considered countries define realisation as the date of delivery, the remaining countries provide a more general definition and recognise revenue when the significant risk of transaction has been transferred to the buyer. Only in Belgium, Denmark and Poland, revenue may be recognised upon execution of a sale contract. Yet, all considered countries determine revenue from the sale of goods on an accrual rather than on a cash basis.

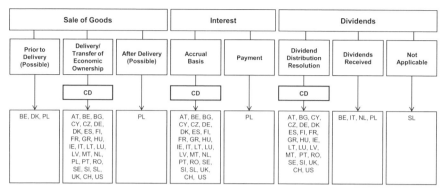

Figure 6: Revenue Recognition and Realisation Dates

A similar picture can be drawn with respect to the realisation date of interest. Interest income is recognised on an accrual basis in all considered countries except Poland, where interest is taxable on a cash basis. Finally, with regard to the recognition of dividend income, 23 of the 28 considered countries recognise dividends as income when declared, i.e. at the time of the dividend distribution resolution. Even though the proposed Council Directive provides no further information in this regard, this is consistent with the general regulations of Article 18. By contrast, in Belgium, Italy, the Netherlands and Poland dividends are taxable to corporate shareholders not until they are received. As dividends are generally exempt the realisation date of dividends is not defined in the Slovakia.

Overall, the determination and recognition of revenue on an accrual basis and the more or less strict application of the realisation principle under the proposed Council Directive follows internationally accepted tax practice. Still, given that the proposed Council Directive does not interfere with financial accounting regulations, e.g. IAS/IFRS, and considering that commercial law is not yet harmonised within the EU, questions arise with respect to the interpretation of the general regulations provided for in Articles 9, 17 and 18. For example, as the vast majority of countries rely on national commercial law to determine the triggering event of revenue recognition, e.g. the transfer of risk, the vague revenue timing criteria under Articles 17 and 18 are likely to yield non-uniform timing of revenues across Member States under a CCCTB. As already mentioned above, it therefore seems advisable to establish a more extensive framework underlying the proposed Council Directive in order to guarantee uniform application of the proposed regulations in all Member States.

C.3.1.2. *Taxation of Unrealised Revenue*

The proposed Council Directive provides for three major exceptions from the general realisation principle as governed by Article 9 (1): Financial assets and liabilities held for trading (Article 23), long-term contracts (Article 24) and income of controlled foreign companies (Article 82).

a) Financial Assets and Liabilities held for Trading

Notwithstanding the general realisation principle described above, Article 23 provides that financial assets held for trading have to be valued on a mark-to-market basis as any differences between the fair market value at the end of the tax year and the fair market value at the beginning of the same tax year are to be included in the tax base (Article 23 (2)). Financial assets or liabilities (Article 4 (15)) are classified as held for trading under the proposed Council Directive if they are (Article 23 (1)):

(1) Acquired or incurred for the purpose of selling or repurchasing in the near term and
(2) Part of a portfolio that is managed together and for which there is evidence of a recent actual pattern of short-term profit-taking.

On the subsequent disposal of financial assets and liabilities the proceeds are to be added to the tax base. Correspondingly, the fair value at the beginning of the tax year or – if later – the market value at the date of purchase, is to be deducted from the tax base (Article 23 (3)).

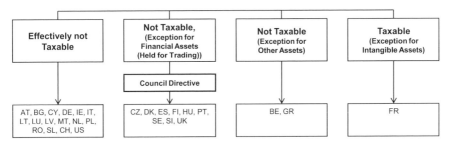

Figure 7: Financial Assets and Liabilities held for Trading (Unrealised Revenue)/ Revaluation Gains

As displayed in Figure 7, revaluation gains are, in principle, not recognised as taxable income in almost all considered countries. In fact, 16 of the 28 considered countries strictly follow the principle of nominal value, i.e. the revaluation of assets beyond acquisition costs is not allowed or any revaluation gains are neutralised by booking unrealised gains to capital reserves. By contrast, revaluation gains, which may arise from the revaluation of depreciable and financial assets, are generally treated as operating profits subject to corporate income tax in France. Yet, in line with the proposed Council Directive, revaluation gains from financial assets (held for trading) are also taxed in the Czech Republic, Denmark, Finland, Hungary, Portugal,[49] Slovenia, Spain, Sweden and the United Kingdom. Furthermore, while a tax effective revaluation of financial assets is generally not allowed, other revalua-

---

[49] Please note that revaluation gains on certain types of biological assets are also taxed in Portugal.

tion gains are taxed in Belgium (capital gains on stock items and work-in-progress) and Greece (revaluation surplus of land and buildings).

Reviewing the regulations of Article 23, similarities to international accounting practice, e.g. IAS 39, are readily identifiable. Against the background of the proceeding implementation of IAS/IFRS in many EU Member States, the taxation of financial assets and liabilities on a fair value base under the proposed Council Directive seems reasonable. Without a formal link to financial accounting regulations, however, several details regarding the practical application of Article 23 still remain open. Most important, common guidelines on how the fair value of financial assets is to be determined when there is no active market are missing.

b) Long-term Contracts

The proposed Council Directive provides special rules regarding revenues and expenses in relation to long-term contracts. According to Article 24 (1), a long-term contract is defined as a contract whose terms exceed 12 months and which is concluded for the purpose of manufacturing, installation and construction, or the performance of services. Notwithstanding the general revenue recognition regulations of Article 18, revenues relating to these contracts are to be recognised based on the percentage-of-completion method. Revenues are, therefore, reported every year by the stage of completion at the end of the tax year. The stage of completion is determined by the ratio of costs to the overall estimated costs or by reference to an expert valuation (Article 24 (2)). Related costs are to be taken into account in the tax year in which they are incurred (Article 24 (3)).

Figure 8 displays the recognition of revenues from long-term contracts in the countries under consideration. In line with the proposed Council Directive the percentage-of-completion method is applied in 13 of the 28 countries under consideration. In addition, 9 countries more or less allow for an option to choose between the percentage-of-completion method and the completed-contract method. The latter does not recognise revenue until all relevant obligations are fulfilled. Nevertheless, in Belgium, this option is only provided for work-in-progress. In addition, Greece, Hungary, Luxembourg, Poland, and Sweden allow the percentage-of-completion method only if the concluded contract includes certain intermediate completion steps. By contrast, Austria, the Czech Republic, France, Germany and Switzerland provide only for the completed-contract method. Finally, Cyprus applies variations of the completed-contract and percentage-of-completion method. Under the "substantially completed method" profits are recognised in the tax year in which the stage of completion reaches 90% of the total contract price. According to the modified percentage-of-completion method, profit is recognised as soon as the stage of completion exceeds 50% of the contract price.

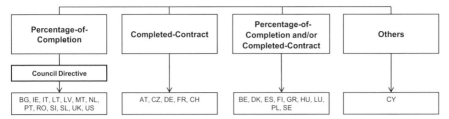

Figure 8: Revenue Recognition from Long-term Contracts

Finally, it is important to note that the proposed Council Directive provides additional rules for reconciling the differences between the treatment of long-term contracts under Article 24 and national tax accounting practice, in order to prevent double or under-taxation on joining the CCCTB. According to Article 46, revenues and expenses relating to long-term contracts are considered to have accrued or been incurred before the taxpayer joins the system but were not yet included in the tax base under the national tax law shall be added to or deducted from the tax base in accordance with the timing rules of national tax law. In addition, revenues which were taxed under the national tax law before joining the group in an amount higher than that which would be included in the tax base under the regulation of Article 24 shall be deducted from the tax base.

c) Controlled Foreign Companies

Notwithstanding the general recognition criteria, the tax base shall include the non-distributed income of an entity resident in a third country if the following conditions of the controlled foreign company regulation (CFC) of Article 82 are met:

(1) Control requirement: The taxpayer holds a direct or indirect participation of more than 50% (voting rights, capital or received profits).
(2) Low tax jurisdiction: Profits are taxable at a corporate tax rate lower than 40% of the average tax rate in the EU or subject to a special regime with a comparably lower level of taxation.
(3) Tainted income: More than 30% of the entity's income falls within specified categories of income in so far as more than 50% of this income can be derived from transactions with the taxpayer or associated companies and consists of interest, royalties, dividends, income from movable or immovable property or income from insurance, banking or other financial activities.
(4) The entity's principal class of shares is not regularly traded on a recognised stock exchange.

By way of exception, such non-distributed income is not included in the tax base under the escape clause of Article 82 (2). Accordingly, non-distributed income is not taxed if the third country is party to the European Economic Area Agreement (EEAA) and if there is an agreement on the exchange of information comparable with the Directive on administrative cooperation.[50]

---

[50] See Council Directive 2011/16/EU of 15.2.2011, 2011 O.J. (L64), p. 1.

If the requirements of Article 82 are fulfilled, not only tainted but all undistributed income is taxable. Article 83 sets the general criteria for the computation of CFC-income under the proposed Council Directive. Accordingly, non-distributed income is only taken into consideration in proportion to the entitlement of the taxpayer's share in the profits (Article 83 (2)) and the amount of income already included in the tax base shall be deducted from the tax base when calculating the taxpayer's liability to tax upon distribution (Article 83 (4)) or the disposal of the shares in a CFC (Article 83 (5)). Losses of the foreign CFC are not included in the tax base (Article 83 (1)) but may be considered in subsequent tax years (loss carryforward). In addition, it should be noted that the general exemption of distributed profits (Article 11) does not apply upon subsequent distribution of CFC-income. As the same low-tax jurisdiction condition as in Article 82 (1) (b) also applies for the general switch-over clause of Article 73, subsequent dividends would be included in the taxpayer's tax base and a credit would be granted for the underlying third country tax (Article 76 (1)).

Figure 9 displays the CFC-regulations and summaries the specific conditions that have to be met in order to be assessed on non-distributed profits in the EU Member States, Switzerland and the US. 12 of the 28 considered countries provide specific CFC-regulations. In short, in line with the proposed Council Directive CFC-regulations apply, if a certain percentage of the capital of the foreign entity is held by a resident taxpayer, the foreign company yields passive income or has no real economic presence in the foreign country and the foreign country is classified as a low tax jurisdiction. Yet, a stock exchange clause as provided for in Article 82 is applied only in the minority of countries, e.g. Hungary or the United Kingdom. Noteworthy, the scope of the CFC-regime in Denmark is broader compared to the CFC-legislation in all other considered countries. It includes all financial subsidiaries in all jurisdictions regardless of the level of taxation.

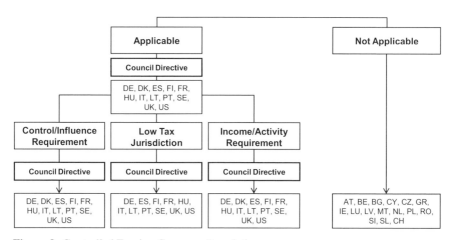

Figure 9: Controlled Foreign Company Regulations

By contrast, Finland, Italy, Lithuania, Sweden and the United Kingdom provide black- or white-lists that assist in determining whether countries are regarded as low tax jurisdictions or not. Although general CFC-regulations are not implemented, tax effective fair value accounting on shareholdings of more than 25% in a non-active company resident in a low tax country is applied in the Netherlands.

To conclude, the CFC-regulations provided by Articles 82 and 83 principally reflect international tax accounting practice. Open questions, however, remain in detail. For example, it remains undefined how the proposed Council Directive would deal with chains of controlled foreign companies in third countries. Most important, however, clear guidance on how to avoid international double taxation if CFC-income is included in the taxpayer's tax base is missing.

C.3.1.3. Capital Gains

Capital gains are considered as ordinary business income under the proposed Council Directive. According to Article 11 (b) and (d), only proceeds from the disposal of shares and pooled assets are tax exempt.[51] For the purpose of calculating a capital gain (or loss), the monetary consideration or the market value in cases where the consideration is non-monetary is to be added to the tax base (Article 22).[52] Correspondingly, the (residual) value for tax purposes incurred in relation to the asset is to be deducted from the tax base in the year of disposal (Article 37 (2)). For non-depreciable assets, the (residual) value for tax purposes comprises the costs of acquisition, construction and improvement (Article 20), adjusted for any exceptional depreciation (Article 37 (2)).

In addition, it is important to note that Article 38 of the proposed Council Directive provides for a rollover relief for replacement assets. If individually depreciable fixed assets (other than assets in the asset pool) which have been owned for at least three years are disposed and the proceeds are to be reinvested within two years in an asset used for the same or similar purposes, the capital gain on the old asset may be rolled over into the costs of the new asset. In other words, the amount by which the proceeds exceed the value for tax purposes is to be deducted from the tax base in the year of disposal and the depreciation base of the replacement asset is correspondingly be reduced by the same amount. Therefore, capital gains taxation is deferred but caught up in the tax years following the purchase of the replacement assets through a reduction in the amount of depreciation. Yet, if a replacement asset is not purchased before the end of the second tax year, the amount formerly deducted is increased by 10% and added to the tax base in the second year after the disposal (Article 38 (2)).

a) Tangible Fixed Assets

As displayed in Figure 10, the majority of countries under consideration are in line with the proposed Council Directive and generally tax capital gains on the disposal of tangible fixed assets as ordinary income. Only in Cyprus, Ireland, Malta, the

---

[51] Please note that tax exempt revenue is discussed in detail in subchapter C.3.2.
[52] Please note that capital losses are discussed in detail in subchapter C.4.1.

United Kingdom and the US, capital gains on the disposal of tangible fixed assets are subject to specific rules. While capital gains are principally tax exempt and, thus, neither subject to corporate income tax nor to any special other capital gains tax in Cyprus,[53] they are subject to separate capital gains tax in Ireland and Malta. In the United Kingdom and the US, separate computational rules for the determination of capital gains and losses apply, but capital gains are subject to corporation tax at the standard tax rates.

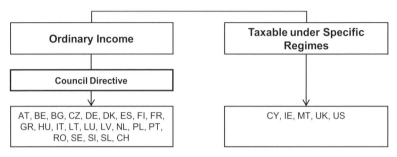

Figure 10: Capital Gains (Tangible Fixed Assets)

b) Intangible Assets

Figure 11 provides an overview of the taxation of capital gains with regard to the disposal of intangible assets. Again, most considered countries are in line with the proposed Council Directive and tax capital gains from the disposal of intangible assets as ordinary business income. In line with the taxation of capital gains on the disposal of tangible fixed assets specific treatment applies in Cyprus, Ireland, Malta, the United Kingdom and the US for the disposal of intangible assets. In addition, such capital gains are subject to special rules in France and the Netherlands. While proceeds from the disposal of patents and patentable inventions benefit from a long-term capital gains regime and a reduced corporate income tax rate in France, self-developed intangibles may be subject to an effective tax rate of 5% in the Netherlands (patent box).

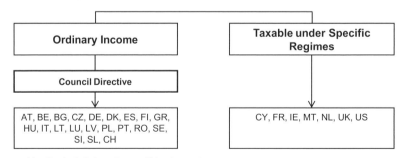

Figure 11: Capital Gains (Intangible Assets)

---

[53] Please note that a capital gains tax at a rate of 20% is imposed only on gains from the disposal of immovable property in Cyprus.

c) Asset Replacement Reserve

As displayed in Figure 12, some form of rollover relief for fixed assets exists in 12 of the 28 countries under consideration. Though, a rollover relief is only provided for certain categories of assets in Germany, Finland, Latvia, Luxembourg, Spain and the United Kingdom. Most restrictive, the German relief merely covers capital gains arising from the sale of land and buildings as well as the produce of agricultural and forestry enterprises.

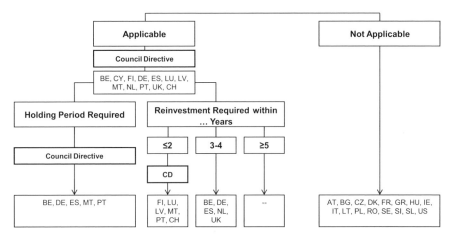

Figure 12: Asset Replacement Reserve / Rollover Relief

Various techniques of providing rollover relief are employed in the countries under consideration. While capital gains on the disposal of fixed assets may be deferred by deducting the gain from both, the tax base and the depreciation base of the replacement asset in most countries under consideration, a partial relief scheme is applicable in Portugal. Accordingly, 50% of capital gains are exempt from tax, provided that the total consideration received is reinvested. Furthermore, Spain applies a reinvestment relief system by granting a tax credit equal to 12% of the gain that arises from a transfer of tangible or intangible fixed assets if all proceeds are reinvested in similar types of assets.

Like the proposed Council Directive, Belgium, Germany, Malta, Portugal and Spain require a minimum holding period between 1 year (Portugal) and 6 years (Germany). With regard to the reinvestment period, Finland, Latvia, Luxembourg, Malta, Portugal and Switzerland[54] are in line with the proposed Council Directive and require that the replacement asset is purchased within 2 years. Belgium, Germany, the Netherlands, Spain and the United Kingdom provide for more generous reinvestment periods ranging between 3 and 4 years. By contrast, no explicit reinvestment period is set in Cyprus.

---

[54] Please note that reinvestment is required within a reasonable timeframe which is considered to be usually between 1 and 3 tax years in Switzerland.

If capital gains are not reinvested within the required time period, they are added back to taxable income in all countries that allow for a rollover relief. The majority of considered countries, however, do not charge any kind of administrative fines or interest payments. In line with the Council Directive, only Belgium, Finland and Germany increase the previously deducted amount in a lump-sum or charge a quasi interest on the taxes saved.

C.3.2. Exempt Revenue

As mentioned above, all revenue is taxable unless explicitly exempt under the proposed Council Directive. The proposed Council Directive lists the following items as exempt revenues (Article 11):

(1) Subsidies directly linked to the acquisition, construction or improvement of fixed assets;
(2) Proceeds from the disposal of pooled assets referred to in Article 39, including the market value of non-monetary gifts;
(3) Received profit distributions;
(4) Proceeds from the disposal of shares; and
(5) Income from a permanent establishment in a third country.

While the first two revenue categories can be classified as temporary exemptions or deferred taxation[55], the last three categories involve genuine exemptions. In this regard, however, one has, to keep in mind that the exemption of revenue received from third country entities is subject to payment of an adequate level of corporate tax in the entity's country of residence or in the country in which the permanent establishment is situated (switch-over clause of Article 73). In short, an entity's country of residence is considered to levy an inadequate level of corporate tax if it provides either for a tax on profits at a statutory corporate tax rate lower than 40% of the average corporate tax rate applicable in the Member States or for a special regime that allows for a substantially lower level of taxation than the general regime. In those cases, profit distributions, capital gains or income from foreign permanent establishments would be taxable under the proposed Council Directive. At the same time, a tax credit is granted on the income that has been taxed in the third country. The credit is apportioned to the group members in the same way as profits (Article 76).

In addition, exempt profit distributions, proceeds from the disposal of shares and income from foreign permanent establishments in a third country may be taken into account when determining the applicable tax rate (Article 72). Obviously, this would be relevant only for those countries applying progressive tax rates on corporate income, e.g. Belgium, Portugal or Spain.

---

[55] While the exempt subsidy is deducted against the depreciation base of the relevant fixed assets, the proceeds from the disposal of pooled assets reduce the balance of the asset pool. Although revenues are exempt, they reduce deductible expenses in future years. For details see subchapters C.3.4.2 and C.3.4.5.

Finally, it is important to note that the deduction of costs incurred in connection with exempt income is, in general terms, not allowed.[56] These costs are fixed at 5% of the exempt income in any given year, unless the taxpayer demonstrates that the actual costs are lower (Article 14 (1) (g)). Effectively, for received profit distributions and capital gains upon the disposal of shares, a 95% exemption rather than a full exemption would apply in most cases.

C.3.2.1. Profit Distributions

For dividends received, the proposed Council Directive includes a uniform approach which exempts received profit distributions in the hands of the recipient irrespective of any minimum shareholding requirement (Article 11 (c)). To avoid double taxation in relation to third countries, both domestic as well as all foreign source dividends are generally exempt under the proposed Council Directive. However, as the international comparison reveals that several distinctions with respect to the taxation of received profit distributions are made in almost all countries under consideration, it is important to distinguish between the taxation of substantial and portfolio ownership interests on the one hand, and domestic and foreign shareholdings on the other hand. Furthermore, mainly due to the implementation of the EU Parent-Subsidiary Directive[57], major differences between the taxation of dividends received from entities resident within the EU or in third countries arise. Yet, in line with the proposed Council Directive, no distinction is made between substantial and portfolio as well as foreign and domestic investments in Cyprus, Germany, Hungary, Italy, Slovakia, Slovenia and the United Kingdom.

a) Profit Distributions from Substantial Shareholding

Domestic Shareholding

As displayed in Figure 13, profit distributions from substantial ownership interest in domestic corporations are, in principle, exempt at the level of corporate shareholders in almost all countries under consideration. Belgium, France, Germany, Italy and Slovenia are in line with the proposed Council Directive and add-back a lump sum of 5% of the dividends to taxable income representing non-deductible business expenses. In 20 of the 28 considered countries, dividends received by another domestic resident company are fully exempt from corporate income tax. In addition, further distribution by the resident parent company is also exempt from distribution tax if a minimum shareholding requirement (10%) is met in Estonia. By contrast, dividends are, in general terms, taxed in the hands of the receiving company in Malta and Spain. Yet, substantial corporate shareholders may qualify for a credit of 100% of the gross dividend derived. In Greece, dividends distributed are subject to withholding tax at a rate of 21%. The withholding tax is final except for certain instances specified by law, e.g. the withholding tax is credited against

---

[56] For details on non-deductible expenses, see subchapter C.3.5.
[57] See Council Directive 90/435/EEC of 23.7.1990, 1990 O. J. (L225), p. 6.

the receiving companies withholding tax for dividends distributed. If the recipient does not distribute profits, the right to offset the tax already withheld is waived.

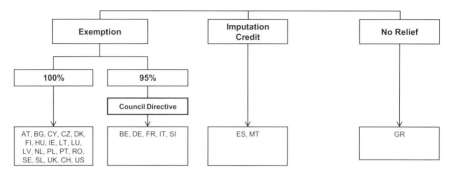

Figure 13: Profit Distributions from Domestic Substantial Shareholding

With the exception of the US, where an 80% ownership level is required for dividends to be fully exempt under the so-called dividend received reduction (DRD), the minimum shareholding required to qualify for preferential tax treatment of dividend income ranges between 5% (e.g. France or the Netherlands) and 10% (e.g. Portugal or Romania). In addition, Belgium, the Czech Republic, France, Luxembourg, Poland, Portugal, Spain and Sweden may require a minimum holding period of up to two years. Finally, a distinction is made between quoted and unquoted shares in Cyprus and Sweden.

Foreign Shareholding

As mentioned above, it is important to distinguish between dividends received from entities resident within or outside the EU. In accordance with the EU Parent-Subsidiary Directive, all EU Member States prevent double taxation of companies on profit distributions received from substantial EU ownership interest either by way of exemption or imputation credit (e.g. Ireland, Malta). Therefore, differences in international tax accounting practice arise mainly with respect to the tax treatment of profit distributions received from entities resident in third-countries.

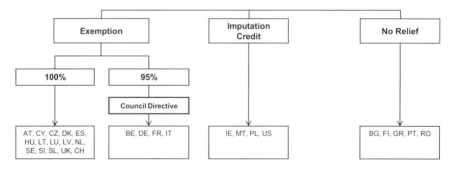

Figure 14: Profit Distributions from Foreign (Non-EU) Substantial Shareholding

In this regard, the majority of countries under consideration unilaterally provide for double taxation relief. In detail, 19 of the 28 considered countries exempt profit distributions received from entities resident outside the EU under certain conditions. Moreover, Ireland, Malta, Poland and the US grant a foreign tax credit. By contrast, third-country profit distributions are included in the corporate income tax base and subject to tax at the general corporate income tax rate in Bulgaria, Portugal and Romania. In Greece, dividends arising from third-countries are also taxed as ordinary income of the resident company and a 20% withholding tax applies. The tax so withheld is credited against the taxpayer's final income tax liability. In addition, foreign-source dividends are fully taxable in Finland; however, a 25% exemption applies if the distributing company is resident in a country with which Finland has a tax treaty.

b) Profit Distributions from Portfolio Shareholding

Domestic Shareholding

Figure 15 provides an overview of the taxation of domestic portfolio dividends. While 14 out of the 28 considered countries are in line with the proposed Council Directive and (substantially) exempt such dividend payments, domestic dividends received from portfolio participations are generally taxed in the remaining 14 countries. In short, domestic portfolio dividends derived by corporate shareholders are fully taxable in Belgium, the Czech Republic, Denmark, France, Greece, the Netherlands, Poland, Portugal and Switzerland. By contrast, Finland (25%), Luxembourg (50%) and the US (70%) provide for a partial exemption relief whereas Malta and Spain apply for a partial credit system.

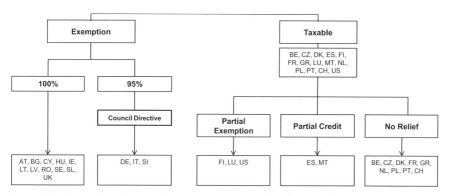

Figure 15: Profit Distributions from Domestic Portfolio Shareholding

Foreign Shareholding

In contrast to dividends derived from foreign substantial or from domestic portfolio investments, relief from double taxation of foreign portfolio dividends is generally not available in the majority of countries under consideration.

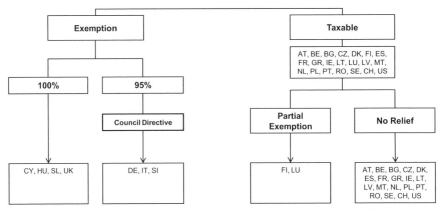

Figure 16: Profit Distributions from Foreign (Non-EU) Portfolio Shareholding

As displayed in Figure 16, 19 of the 28 countries under consideration do neither exempt foreign portfolio dividends nor credit the underlying foreign taxes (as opposed to credit for tax withheld, which is creditable in all countries except for Switzerland). By contrast, Cyprus, Germany, Hungary, Italy, Slovakia, Slovenia and the United Kingdom are in line with the proposed Council Directive and (substantially) exempt profit distributions in the hands of the receiving company irrespective of whether they are distributed by entities resident within or outside the EU. It is noteworthy that foreign portfolio dividends are also exempt from corporate income tax in Austria and Bulgaria if they are received from EU Member State entities. In addition, Finland and Luxembourg partially exempt foreign portfolio dividends in the hands of the resident recipient if they are paid by an entity resident in the EU or in a country with which a tax treaty exists.

C.3.2.2. Capital Gains upon the Disposal of Shares

In line with the proposed Council Directive, profit distributions on the one hand, and profit retention with subsequent sale of the shares on the other hand, are taxed equally in several countries under consideration, e.g. in Germany, Italy or Switzerland. Yet, while there is, again, no minimum shareholding requirement for the general exemption of capital gains upon the disposal of shares under the proposed Council Directive (Article 11 (d)), substantial and portfolio as well as foreign and domestic shareholdings have to be considered separately for the purpose of the international comparison. Only Bulgaria, Cyprus, Germany, Italy, Poland, Portugal, Romania, Slovakia and the US differentiate neither between substantial and portfolio nor foreign and domestic shareholdings.

a) Disposal of Substantial Shareholdings

Domestic Shareholding

Capital gains realised upon the disposal of domestic substantial ownership interest in corporations are either partially or fully exempt from tax, subject to a reduced tax rate or can be deferred.[58] As displayed in Figure 17, (substantial) exemption is – in line with the proposed Council Directive – granted in 18 of the 28 countries under consideration.[59] Again, Estonia docs not tax capital gains when they are earned, as only distributed profits are subject to tax. Furthermore, a partial exemption (50%) is provided for in Slovenia if the shareholding represents a participation of at least 8%, the shares have been held for at least 6 months and at least one person was employed during the holding period. Similar requirements can be found in almost all other countries granting tax exemption. For example, 10 countries require a minimum holding period between one (e.g. Belgium, the Czech Republic, Finland or Switzerland) and two years (e.g. France or Lithuania). Furthermore, almost all countries require a minimum shareholding requirement between 5% (e.g. Ireland or the Netherlands) and 30% in Hungary.

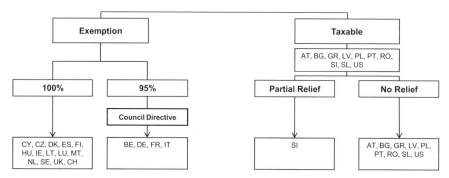

Figure 17: Disposal of Substantial Domestic Shareholdings

By contrast, 9 countries provide no general tax relief on the disposal of substantial domestic ownership interests in corporations. However, it is worth mentioning that capital gains on the disposal of shares are also tax exempt in Bulgaria, Greece and Latvia if these shares are publicly traded on a regulated stock market in the European Economic Area (EEA).

Foreign Shareholding

As displayed in Figure 18, (substantial) exemption is – in line with the treatment of domestic shareholdings – also granted for foreign substantial shareholdings in the majority of countries under consideration. Notably, while no tax relief applies to capital gains from the disposal of a participation in a resident company, capital gains derived from the disposal of a foreign shareholding are exempt under the conditions of the international participation exemption (e.g. a holding period of at least one year) in Austria.[60]

---

[58] For deferred taxation, see the discussion on asset replacement reserves in subchapter C.3.1.3.

[59] Please note that capital gains from the disposal of shares in private companies which own domestic immovable property are not exempt in Cyprus.

[60] Please note that an exemption applies in Austria unless the resident company has exercised an option to treat capital gains as taxable income.

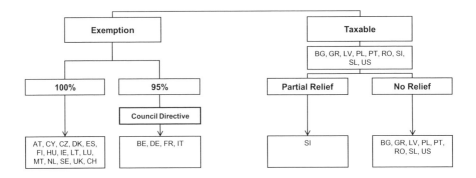

Figure 18: Disposal of Substantial Foreign (Non-EU) Shareholdings

Contrary to the treatment of dividends received from substantial foreign share-holdings, double taxation relief applies not only to foreign-source capital gains on the sale of shares in a company resident within the EU, but also for third-country investments. For third-country investments, additional requirements may, however, apply. For example, unilateral relief on capital gains in the Czech Republic, Finland or Lithuania is granted only if the company whose shares are disposed of is resident in a third-country with which a tax treaty is in force.

As for domestic shareholdings, certain holding and minimum shareholding requirements have to be met in order to qualify for exemption in almost all countries under consideration. Furthermore, in line with the switch-over clause of the proposed Council Directive that makes provision for a change from the exemption method to the credit method in the case of low taxation of the third-country company (Article 73), a minimum foreign tax rate is required in several countries under consideration. For example, the exemption method is not granted to the extent that the foreign tax rate falls below a minimum tax rate of 12% in the Czech Republic whereas in Italy the company must be a resident of a state or territory which is included in the white-list provided by the Ministry of Finance.

b) Disposal of Portfolio Shares

As displayed in Figure 19, the number of countries that provide a tax relief on the disposal of portfolio shares is rather small compared to the disposal of substantial ownership interest. Only Cyprus,[61] Germany and Italy are in line with the proposed Council Directive and provide for a general exemption of capital gains derived by corporate shareholders. This holds true for both capital gains realised from the sale of shares in domestic and foreign companies. Nevertheless, as unquoted shares are always deemed to be business-related holdings, exemption is also granted for unquoted shares in Sweden. In addition, capital gains on the disposal of portfolio shares are tax exempt in Bulgaria, Greece and Latvia under the condition that the shares are publicly traded on a regulated stock market in the EEA.

---

[61] Please note that capital gains from the disposal of shares in private companies which own domestic immovable property are not exempt in Cyprus.

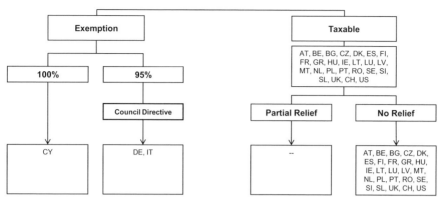

Figure 19: Disposal of Portfolio Shareholdings

C.3.2.3. Income of a Foreign Permanent Establishment

Income of a permanent establishment in a third country is exempt from corporate tax under the proposed Council Directive (Article 11 (e)). Article 5 defines the term permanent establishment, which is, in general terms, consistent with the OECD Model Tax Convention. As already mentioned above, the proposed Council Directive provides, however, for a switch-over from exemption to taxation under the conditions of the switch-over regulation of Article 73. In this regard, the taxable income of the foreign permanent establishment shall be determined in accordance with the rules of the proposed Council Directive. Yet, it is worth mentioning that the exemptions provided for in Article 11 (e) would not affect permanent establishments in other Member States, as those permanent establishments would be treated as if they were members of the group (Article 4 (7)).

Although 9 of the 28 countries under consideration are in line with the proposed Council Directive and exempt (with progression) income derived through a foreign permanent establishment under certain conditions (e.g. minimum foreign tax rate), income of foreign permanent establishments is generally subject to tax in the vast majority of countries under consideration (Figure 20). Yet, taxpayers may credit foreign taxes on the permanent establishment's income against their national tax on the foreign-source income in almost all countries under considerations. Only in Slovakia, there is no unilateral tax relief available. In addition, in line with the OECD Model Tax Convention, most considered countries grant partial or complete exemption bilaterally at the level of double tax treaties.

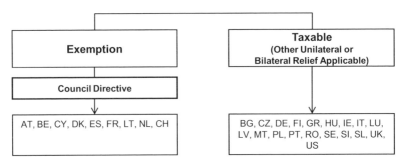

Figure 20: Income of Foreign Permanent Establishment

To conclude, the avoidance of double taxation of foreign income by the strict application of the exemption method under the proposed Council Directive is to be welcomed as it is able to resolve many of the double taxation problems arising in cross-border activities. Yet, a lack of detailed guidance remains with respect to the switch-over rule of Article 73, e.g. unclear definition (e.g. what regimes are considered special for purposes of Article 73) or several details on computing the credit under Article 76 are missing. In particular, the relationship between existing tax treaties providing for tax exemption and the switch-over rule of Article 73 has to be clarified, although it is understood that such treaties will override the rules of the proposed Council Directive. Furthermore, it seems advisable to include a detailed definition of dividends qualifying for exemption. In particular, clear guidance on the treatment of deemed dividends is missing. With regard to the treatment of foreign permanent establishments, common rules on the determination of the amount of exempt income, i.e. the allocation of income to foreign permanent establishments, are still to be established. In addition, the proposed Council Directive remains silent on the treatment of losses incurred in foreign permanent establishments.

C.3.3. Deductible Expenses

As a general rule, income tax is imposed on revenue reduced by deductible expenses and other deductible items under the proposed Council Directive (Article 10). The fundamental concept underlying the definition of deductible expenses is laid down in Article 12. According to Article 12, all costs of sales and expenses net of deductible value added tax incurred by the taxpayer with a view of obtaining or securing income qualify as deductible expenses.[62] Private expenses are not deductible. Although this general principle constitutes the main criteria for the deduction of expenses in all considered countries, the detailed implementation differs. At the heart of these differences are questions regarding the valuation (e.g. the initial measurement of costs) and the timing (e.g. the treatment of bad debt receivables) of relevant business expenses. Another important example for differences is account-

---

[62] Please note that the proposed Council Directive distinguishes between expenses that reduce taxable income of the current period and capital expenditures. The latter are, in general, taken into account as other deductible items and are discussed in detail in subchapter C.3.4.

ing for provisions (e.g. provisions for pensions). Finally, important differences arise in distinguishing between productive / deductible expenses and private / non-deductible expenses. In this respect, the proposed Council Directive provides a comprehensive list of non-deductible expenses in Article 14.[63]

In order to avoid double counting or undercounting of expenses due to the transition from national tax accounting to the proposed CCCTB, the proposed Council Directive provides special transitional rules in Article 47. To the extent that expenses incurred in relation to activities carried out before joining the proposed CCCTB have not been deducted, expenses shall be deducted under the proposed Council Directive (Article 47 (2)). By contrast, amounts already deducted may not be deducted again (Article 47 (3)).

C.3.3.1. General Principles and Timing of Expenses

As discussed above, Article 17 is central to the determination of taxable income under the proposed Council Directive. Stating that deductible expenses are to be recognised in the tax year in which they are incurred, it sets the general criteria for the allocation and timing of expenses. Article 19 further specifies that a deductible expense is incurred when the following three conditions are met: First, the obligation to make a payment has arisen. Second, the amount of the obligation can be quantified with reasonable accuracy. And third, the significant risks and rewards of ownership over goods have been transferred (trade in goods) or services have been received by the taxpayer (supply of services) respectively.

With regard to the general principles and timing of expenses in the countries under consideration, it first has to be emphasised that the timing of expenses generally follows the treatment under financial accounts. As mentioned above and displayed in Figure 5, the accrual basis of accounting is hence central to all considered tax systems. Accordingly, deductible expenses are, regardless of payment, incurred when the obligation to make the payment has arisen and the related amount is either known or objectively determinable.

Major differences between the proposed Council Directive and national tax practice, therefore, cannot be found in the general principles underlying the recognition and timing of expenses. Rather, differences between the national tax practice and the proposed Council Directive arise with respect to the implementation and the extent of deviations from these general principles, all of which will be discussed in the following.

C.3.3.2. Stocks and Work-in-Progress

According to Article 21, the total amount of deductible expenses is to be increased by the value of stocks and work-in-progress at the beginning of the tax year and reduced by the value of stocks and work-in-progress at the end of the same tax year. Thus, a primary issue in determining the total amount of deductible expenses is the determination of the value at which stock items and work-in-progress are carried at

---

[63] For details on non-deductible expenses, see subchapter C.3.5.

the beginning and the end of the tax year. In short, three questions concerning the valuation of inventories have to be answered: First, which method should be used for the initial measurement of the costs of stock items and work-in-progress? Second, is an individual measurement for the costs of each item of stock and work-in-progress required or are any simplifying valuation methods applicable? And third, how is the value of stocks and work-in-progress determined at the end of the tax year (subsequent measurement)?

Initial Measurement

Under the proposed Council Directive, the initial costs of stock items and work-in-progress comprises all costs of purchase, direct costs of conversion and other direct costs incurred in bringing inventories to their present location and conditions (Article 29 (2)). Indirect costs on conversion, such as fixed and variable overheads, or other indirect costs (e.g. interest and other borrowing costs) are not included in the costs of inventories. Although the proposed Council Directive allows only for the direct cost approach, Article 29 (2) provides an important exception for taxpayers who included indirect costs before opting for the CCCTB. In contrast to the general rule of Article 29 (2), those taxpayers are entitled to continue to apply the indirect cost approach.

While the proposed Council Directive specifically defines the costs of stock items and work-in-progress in Article 29 (2), most EU Member States as well as Switzerland and the US generally do not distinguish between the initial measurement of stock items and other assets.[64] All manufactured goods have to be valued at production costs and acquired items have to be valued at acquisition cost. Even though all considered countries, hence, require inventories to be valued at historical costs at the time of purchase or production, there are extensive differences in the understanding of the measurement of costs.[65]

Acquisition Costs

As mentioned above, the determination of acquisition costs under the proposed Council Directive generally follows the direct cost approach. Thus, the acquisition costs of stock items and work-in-progress comprises all costs of purchase, direct costs of conversion and other direct costs incurred in bringing the stock items to their present location and condition (Article 29 (2)).

---

[64] For the valuation of fixed assets under the Council Directive, see Article 33 of the Council Directive and subchapter C.3.4.4.

[65] Please note that the costs related to work-in-progress are not capitalised in the Netherlands but are deductible when incurred. Instead, a pro rata part of the contract price is capitalised.

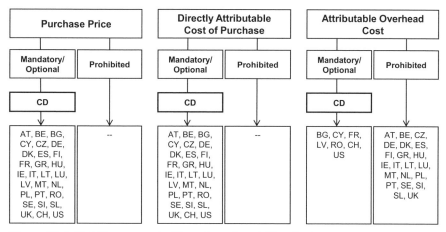

Figure 21: Initial Measurement of Inventory: Acquisition Cost

Figure 21 displays the main components of costs that must be included in the considered countries when determining the acquisition costs of stocks and work-in-progress. In line with the proposed Council Directive, all EU Member States, Switzerland and the US require acquisition costs to include the purchase price and all direct attributable costs of purchase less trade discounts and rebates. Differences arise, however, with respect to directly attributable overheads. While the proposed Council Directive as well as Bulgaria, Cyprus, France, Latvia, Romania, Switzerland and the US require directly attributable overheads to be included in the initial value of stocks and work-in-progress, the remaining EU Member States generally prohibit the capitalisation of overhead costs.

Production Cost

Article 29 (2) does not distinguish between acquisition and production cost. The value of produced stock items and work-in-progress shall include all direct costs of conversion and other direct costs incurred in bringing inventories to their present location and conditions. Consequently, inventory costs neither include indirect material and production overhead (e.g. depreciation of fixed assets; general administration cost) nor distribution costs.

While the proposed Council Directive generally allows for the capitalisation of direct costs only, Figure 22 reveals that almost all considered countries follow a full cost approach or, at least permit it as an option. Yet, there are major differences in the definition of full cost. For example, while most countries prohibit distribution costs to be included in full cost, Belgium, Bulgaria and Malta require or allow capitalisation of these costs. In addition, while 11 out of the 28 countries under consideration are in line with the proposed Council Directive and prohibit the capitalisation of administrative cost, 17 countries require or allow them to be taken into account if they are related to the production process.

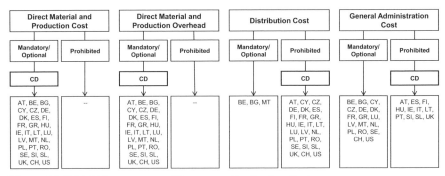

Figure 22: Initial Measurement of Inventory: Production Cost

At this point, it has to be emphasised that the definition of the initial costs of stocks and work-in-progress under Article 29 (2) must be seen as a first rough idea of what is to be measured at costs of inventory under the proposed CCCTB.[66] The comparison of the proposed Council Directive with national tax regulations reveals that many details (e.g. a clear distinction between direct and indirect costs or an in-depth definition of individual cost components) are not provided. Furthermore, while the option to include indirect costs obviously is intended to reduce administrative complexity when entering the CCCTB system, it is at least questionable whether the deviation from a uniform treatment would take away some of the administrative advantages of the CCCTB project.

Simplifying Valuation Methods

According to Article 29 (1), the costs of stock items and work-in-progress that are not ordinarily interchangeable and goods or services produced and segregated for specific projects are to be measured individually. Other goods or services may be measured by applying the first in first out (FiFo) or the weighted-average cost method.

FiFo assumes that the items of stock and work-in-progress which were purchased or produced first are consumed or sold first. Consequently, the items remaining at the end of the tax year are those most recently purchased or produced. According to the weighted-average cost method, the costs of each item are determined by the weighted average of the costs of similar items at the beginning of the tax year and the costs of similar items produced or purchased during the tax year.

---

[66]   See also Kahle/Schulz (2011), p. 296.

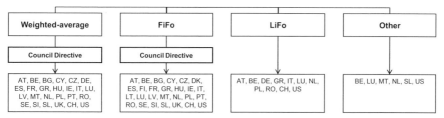

Figure 23: Stocks and Work-in-Progress: Simplifying Valuation Methods

In most countries under consideration, tax legislation refers to the treatment under financial accounts and does not provide separate regulations for tax purposes. As displayed in Figure 23, FiFo as well as the weighted-average cost method are in this regard widely accepted. While 25 of the 28 countries allow for the weighted-average cost method, 27 out of the 28 considered countries accept FiFo for tax purposes. Besides these two methods, LiFo is accepted in 11 of the considered countries. LiFo assumes that the items sold were those most recently purchased. In general, countries allowing for all three of the mentioned methods set one method as preference or require the method which best reflects the underlying transactions. Furthermore, Belgium, Luxembourg, Malta, the Netherlands, Slovakia and the US allow other valuation methods, such as HiFo (e.g. Luxembourg) or the base-stock method (e.g. the Netherlands), depending on the circumstances.

Subsequent Measurement

Article 29 (4) provides that stock items and work-in-progress are required to be valued on the last day of the tax year at the lower of cost and net realisable value. While the determination of costs is discussed in detail above (initial measurement), the net realisable value is defined as the estimated selling price in the ordinary course of business less the estimated costs of completion and the estimated costs necessary to make the sale. In line with Article 21, any write-down to the net realisable value is recognised as a deductible expense in the period in which the decrease in value occurs. Consequently, any reversal in the net realisable value is added back to taxable income in the period in which the reversal occurs.

The results displayed in Figure 24 reveal that Article 21 generally coincides with the general practice of the national tax regulations in most instances. Items of stock and work-in-progress are usually written down to the lower market value in 20 of the 28 considered countries if they are subject to diminution in value due to damage, spoilage, obsolescence or lower demand. Only Bulgaria, the Czech Republic, Latvia, Lithuania, Malta, Poland, Romania and Slovakia prohibit an adjustment to the lower of cost or market value and strictly account for stock items and work-in-progress at historic costs.

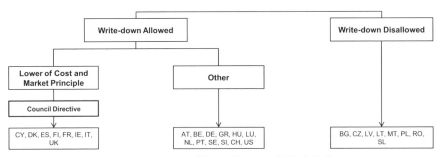

Figure 24: Subsequent Measurement of Stock Items and Work-in-Progress

Even though the majority of the considered countries recognise lost value of stock items and work-in-progress as deductible expenses, discrepancies arise with respect to the determination of the market value. 8 of the 28 considered countries are more or less in line with the proposed Council Directive and define the market value as the net realisable value, i.e. an estimated selling price in the ordinary course of business less the estimated costs of completion and the estimated costs necessary to make the sale. By contrast, 12 countries write down stock items and work-in-progress to replacement costs determined by reference to the procurement market or stipulate other deviations from the strict lower of cost and market principle as provided in the proposed Council Directive.

C.3.3.3. Bad Debt Receivables

Article 27 provides that a specific deduction from the tax base should be allowed for bad debt receivables where, in short, the taxpayer has taken all reasonable steps to pursue payments and reasonably believes that the debt will not be satisfied. In addition, Article 27 (1) includes a general provision allowing for a deduction from taxable income if the taxpayer has a large number of homogeneous receivables and is able to reliably estimate the amount of the bad debt receivable on a percentage basis.

While the proposed Council Directive generally allows for both specific and general provisions to account for bad debt receivables, many countries limit the deductibility of costs for bad debts to specific provisions, i.e. the deductible amount is determined based on reviewing the individual trade debtor owing to the corporation. Thus, in analysing whether the national tax regulations of the considered countries are in line with the Council Directive, it is important to distinguish between both types of provisions.

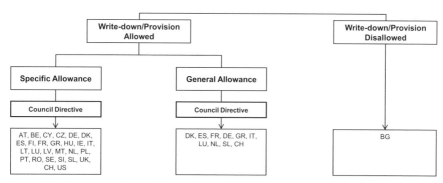

Figure 25: Accounting for Bad Debt Receivables

Figure 25 shows that almost all EU Member States, Switzerland and the US permit specific provisions or specific deductions for bad debts under certain conditions, e.g. the receivables are overdue for a certain number of months or the taxpayer has unsuccessfully attempted to recover a debt and documentary evidence proves such attempts. Only in Bulgaria, write-downs of bad or doubtful receivables are generally not tax-deductible. Accordingly, bad debt receivables are not deductible in Bulgaria until the statute of limitation expires or the insolvency proceedings against the debtor have been closed.

In addition, Denmark, France, Germany, Greece, Italy, Luxembourg, the Netherlands, Slovakia, Spain[67] and Switzerland are in line with the proposed Council Directive and allow for general provisions under certain conditions. In doing so, the deductible amount is generally calculated as a percentage of total sales / turnover (e.g. Greece), of all debts not covered by guarantees (e.g. Italy) or of all overdue amounts (e.g. Slovakia) and / or must be based on past experience (e.g. Luxembourg).

Regarding the treatment of bad debt receivables on transition from national tax law to the proposed CCCTB, Article 47 (1) provides that bad debt deductions are to be deductible only to the extent that they arise from activities or transactions carried out after the taxpayer joins the systems. Yet, the proposed Council Directive does not provide guidance on the treatment of differences in valuing such receivables. Whether the general rule on recognition and valuation provided by Article 44 is applicable, remains somewhat unclear.

C.3.3.4. Provisions

Article 25 defines the requirements for provisions in order to be – notwithstanding the general principles of Article 19 – tax deductible under the proposed Council Directive. Accordingly, provisions are recognised under the proposed Council Directive only when there is a legal obligation or a probable legal obligation arising

---

[67] In Spain, the allowance is restricted to taxable entities which are taxed under the special scheme for „small-sized entities", i.e. entities with revenue of less than EUR 10 million in the preceding taxable period.

from activities or transactions carried out in or before the tax year. Yet, provisions for payments that the taxpayer expects to make voluntarily, e.g. provisions for deferred repair and maintenance, are not allowed. Furthermore, Article 25 (1) states that the amounts arising from those legal obligations have to be reliably assessable and that the eventual settlement is expected to result in a deductible expense. For those obligations relating to activities which continue in future tax years, the deduction is spread proportionately over the estimated duration.

Article 25 (2) governs the measurement of provisions. In short, provisions are to be measured at the expected expenditure required to settle the obligation at the end of the tax year provided that the estimate is based on all relevant factors, e.g. the past experience of the company or industry. In reaching the estimate, the following elements are to be taken into account:

(1) All risks and uncertainties;
(2) Future events and benefits that can reasonably be expected to occur, i.e. price increases have to be reflected in the recognised amount; and
(3) Future benefits directly linked to the event giving rise to the provision.

Furthermore, provisions have to be discounted at the yearly average of the Euro Interbank Offered Rate (Euribor) for obligations with a maturity of 12 months or a different agreed rate.

Finally, provisions are to be reviewed and adjusted at the end of each tax year. If the obligation is no longer probable, its amount has to be reversed to income.

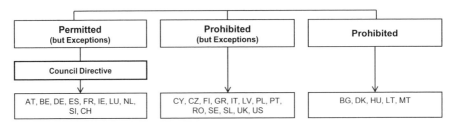

Figure 26: Recognition of Provisions: General Principles

As displayed in Figure 26, only 10 of the 28 considered countries permit the recognition of provisions. The other 18 countries generally prohibit a tax-effective deduction for provisions. The reason is that tax systems which are closer to cash-flow taxation – like the tax accounting in the US – tend to recognise provisions only when the payment is made. Nevertheless, 13 out of these 18 countries, among them Italy, the United Kingdom and the US, allow for certain exceptions to the general rule.

Figure 27 displays the treatment of different categories of provisions under the proposed Council Directive and the national tax practice in all considered countries.[68] Most notably, provisions for contingent losses are expected to be within the scope of Article 25.[69]

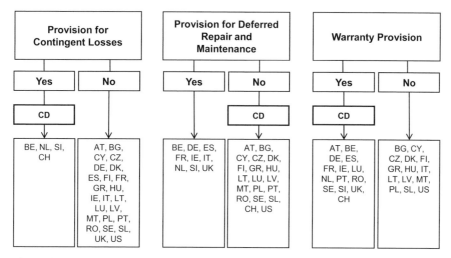

Figure 27: Recognition of Provisions: Different Categories

While most of the considered countries prohibit provisions for contingent losses for tax purposes, Belgium, the Netherlands, Slovenia and Switzerland are in line with the proposed Council Directive. A similar picture can be drawn for warranty provisions satisfying the requirements for provisions under the proposed Council Directive and in 14 of the 28 considered countries. In contrast, provisions for deferred repair and maintenance are prohibited under the proposed Council Directive as they constitute future payments for which the taxpayer has no legal obligation. In this regard, 9 countries, e.g. Germany, France and Spain, are less restrictive and allow for certain provisions for which the taxpayer is not legally obligated, e.g. for deferred repair or maintenance.

Referring to the 10 countries which generally allow the recognition of provisions under their national tax regulations, Figure 28 also reveals a great disparity in the measurement of provisions under the proposed Council Directive and national tax accounting practice. While all of these countries as well as the proposed Council Directive require that the estimation of provisions is based on past experience,[70]

---

[68] Figure 27 also highlights that special provisions are allowed in more than the 10 countries generally permitting the recognition of provisions.

[69] Same opinion Scheffler/Krebs (2011), p. 22; Kahle/Schulz (2011), pp. 301 f.

[70] In Ireland, the recognition of provisions is based on the accounting concept. The tax code does not specify the precise methodology to be used in measuring provisions. Once the provisions are properly measured under Irish/UK GAAP or IFRS, the tax consequences follow there from.

measurements of provisions are based on discounted present values only in 5 of the 10 countries. In Austria,[71] Ireland, the Netherlands and Slovenia, no statutory discount rate is provided for by law; rather, a rate that reflects the current market conditions and the risks specific to the provision should be applied. In contrast, a statutory rate of 5.5% is stipulated in Germany. Furthermore, all considered countries except France and the Netherlands are in line with the Council Directive and take into account future benefits linked to the event giving rise to the provision.

Finally, reviews and taxable adjustments of provisions at the end of each tax year are mandatory – or at least optionally permitted – in 9 of the 10 countries which generally allow for tax-deductible provisions. Only Switzerland generally neglects adjustments of provisions for tax purposes.

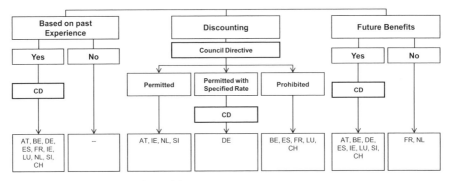

Figure 28: Measurement of Provisions

At this point, it has to be emphasised that the proposed Council Directive provides detailed recognition and measurement criteria regarding provisions. Yet, some open questions remain.[72] Most important, clarification is needed with respect to provisions for contingent losses. While provisions for contingent losses may not be recorded for tax purposes in most of the EU Member States, it is questionable whether contingent losses fall under the criteria of Article 25, i.e. whether contingent losses would be classified as an obligation that arose from transactions carried out in the current or previous tax year.[73] Further questions arise as neither authoritative interpretation of the proposed Council Directive nor a formal link to financial accounting practice is available yet. Thus certain requirements and legal terms of Article 25, e.g. the minimum probability requirement (probability percentage) or the kind of future developments taken into account when measuring provisions (e.g. inflation) remain vague and / or incomplete. In this respect, more detailed rules for the recognition and measurement of different classes of provisions need to be developed. In addition, the strict requirement of a legal obligation is a controversial issue. From a mere economic perspective, provisions should also be admitted

---

[71] Provisions in Austria are not discounted; however, only 80% of the expenses are considered tax deductible.

[72] See also European Economic and Social Committee (2011), p. 8.

[73] See Scheffler/Krebs (2011), p. 22.

in case of constructive obligations, e.g. if there is an established pattern of past practice. Clearly, the Commission seeks to impose a level of objectivity by limiting the recognition of provisions to legal obligations; however, drawing a sophisticated and clear line between legal and pure constructive obligations is not without its problems. For example, it remains unclear whether the announcement of a social compensation plan fulfils the requirement of a legal obligation. Again, authoritative interpretation and clear guidance is needed.

Finally, it is important to note that Article 47 aims to prevent that provisions are deducted twice due to the transition from national tax law to the proposed CCCTB. In short, Article 47 (1) stipulates that additions to provisions are only deductible under the proposed Council Directive to the extent that they arise from activities or transactions carried out after joining the CCCTB system. In addition, expenses incurred in relation to transactions carried out before the taxpayer opted into the system but for which no deduction had been made are deductible under the proposed Council Directive (Article 47 (2)). Furthermore, Article 44 provides for the rollover of existing tax book values of provisions at the time the option to join the proposed CCCTB is exercised. Yet, the proposed Council Directive does not provide more guidance on how to handle existing differences in recognising and valuing provisions.

C.3.3.5. Pension Payments

In general, there are two distinct ways to provide post employment benefits. First, pension obligations might be funded by payments to an external pension fund, e.g. an insurance company or another organisation (indirect pension plans). Contributions to the fund – as incurred by the taxpayer with a view of obtaining or securing – are deductable under the proposed Council Directive (Article 12). Second, companies may choose to pay benefits directly with or without pension provisions set up in advance (direct pension plans). In this regard, Article 26 complements the general rules governed by Article 25 and provides supplementary regulations in order to determine the amount of pension provisions. Most important, according to Article 25 actuarial techniques are to be used. Just as general provisions, pension provisions are also discounted by reference to the annual average of Euribor for obligations with a maturity of 12 months.

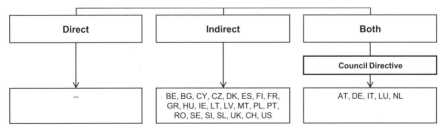

Figure 29: Deductibility of Pension Payments

As displayed in Figure 29, indirect pension plans are more or less common in all EU Member States, Switzerland and the US. Furthermore, all countries under consideration are in line with the proposed Council Directive and treat contributions to external pension funds as tax deductible expenses.[74] By contrast, although direct pension schemes can be found in other countries under consideration, e.g. France and Hungary,[75] only Austria, Germany, Italy, Luxembourg and the Netherlands grant tax deductions for allocations to pension provisions.

Regarding the measurement of pension provisions, Italian and Luxembourgian tax accounting rules refer to local GAAP. In contrast, autonomous tax law regulations are provided in Austria, Germany and the Netherlands. Yet, all 5 countries prescribe a clearly defined evaluation method (so-called accumulation method and uniform distribution approach) to measure pension provisions. In line with the proposed Council Directive specified rates to discount pension provisions are used in all 5 countries. While the interest rate in Austria and Germany is fixed at 6%, accounting regulations in Luxembourg prescribe a discount rate of 5%. In the Netherlands an actuarial discount rate of at least 4% is prescribed. In contrast, only Italy is in line with the proposed Council Directive taking future events, e.g. increases in salary, into account when measuring pension provisions.[76]

Open questions remain with respect to the detailed measurement of pension provisions. Similarly to the general provisions under Article 25, detailed criteria for a reliable estimate are not specified by Article 26. Neither is a particular technique for the determination of pension provisions provided nor does the proposed Council Directive contain any specific information regarding the underlying determinants. In this respect, clarification is needed in order to ensure uniform treatment in all Member States. Furthermore, although the prescription of an explicit discount rate is appropriate to achieve uniform application of tax accounting practice across Member States, the application of a short-term discount rate, i.e. the Euribor for obligations with a maturity of 12 months, is questionable. Considering the long-term character of pensions, a long-term discount rate seems to be more appropriate in this respect.

Finally, in line with the treatment of general provisions, Article 44 and Article 47 (1) provide transitional rules for pension provisions. Again, the main principle of entry is the rollover of existing tax book values. Furthermore, Article 47 (1) stipulates that additions to pension provisions are only deductible under the proposed Council Directive to the extent that they arise from activities carried out after joining the CCCTB system.

---

[74] Currently, the state pension, which is tax-deductable, is the only pension scheme recognised in Malta.

[75] In these countries, tax deduction is not available until the pension payment falls due. In Slovenia, direct pension promises are partly deductible.

[76] Please note that Luxembourg GAAP does not provide any specific rules or guidelines on how to measure a provision for pension obligations. Therefore, it is difficult to precisely specify the treatment of pension provisions in Luxembourg.

C.3.4. Other Deductible Items

As mentioned above, the proposed Council Directive strictly distinguishes between expenses that reduce taxable income of the current period (deductible expenses) and capital expenditures. The latter are taken into account as other deductible items and are discussed in the following subchapter.

In general, Article 13 provides that a proportional deduction from the tax base may be made with respect to the depreciation of fixed assets. Fixed assets are defined in Article 4 (14). Accordingly, fixed assets comprise tangible and acquired intangible assets which are capable of being valued independently, secure income for more than 12 months and are used in the business for the production, maintenance or securing of income for more than 12 months.

One of the core debates surrounding the depreciation of fixed assets raised by the European Commission in preliminary stages of the CCCTB project has focused on the question whether assets are to be depreciated on an individual or a pool basis. In this regard, the proposed Council Directive provides an interim solution. In detail, it sets out two different systems of depreciation of fixed assets. While Article 36 prescribes individual straight-line depreciation for buildings, tangible assets with a useful life of over 15 years and intangibles, tangible assets with a useful life of less than 15 years are taken together in an asset pool, which is depreciated at a rate of 25%. Therefore, after discussing the general principles, the determination of the depreciation base and the treatment of low-value assets under the proposed Council Directive, we focus on the two different systems of depreciation and describe individual depreciable assets and the asset pool as governed in Article 39 separately. Finally, exceptional depreciation for assets which have permanently decreased in value is discussed.

C.3.4.1. General Principles

Regarding the general principles underlying the depreciation of assets, two distinct questions have to be answered: First, who is entitled to depreciation? In this respect, Article 34 designates the economic owner to be entitled to depreciation. Only if the economic owner of an asset cannot be identified, the legal owner is permitted to depreciate the assets. Article 4 (20) defines the economic owner as the person who has substantially all the benefits and risks attached to a fixed asset, regardless of whether that person is the legal owner. In addition, a taxpayer who has the right to possess, use and dispose of a fixed asset and bears the risk of its loss or destruction is to be considered the economic owner in any event.

Second, the timing of the depreciation has to be settled. Most important, the treatment of assets acquired or disposed of during the year has to be clarified. In this respect, Article 37 sets out a full year's depreciation in the year of acquisition or entry into use, whichever comes later. Accordingly, no depreciation is to be deducted in the year of disposal.

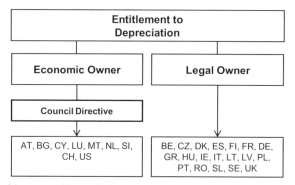

Figure 30: Entitlement to Depreciation

As displayed in Figure 30, 19 of the 28 considered countries are not in line with the proposed Council Directive and, in general terms, classify the legal owner as being entitled to depreciation. The legal owner is, in short, defined as the taxpayer that has an enforceable claim or right to an asset and is recognised as such by commercial law. Referring to the timing of depreciation, depreciation is permitted at acquisition or entry to use in all countries under consideration. In addition, depreciation in Spain may also begin when revenues are generated by the underlying asset. In contrast to the proposed Council Directive, assets acquired during the year are depreciated based on a pro rata temporis basis in most of the considered countries, i.e. depreciation is deducted in the proportion to the length of time involved (e.g. month by month) or full annual depreciation charge is reduced on a lump-sum basis. For example, the Czech Republic, Denmark, Finland and Malta allow for a full year's depreciation in the year of acquisition.

Overall, the proposed Council Directive provides a detailed framework with respect to the general principles of depreciation; however, it has to be noted that further elaborations seem to be necessary in order to create uniform treatment in all 27 Member States. Considering that commercial law is to date not harmonised within the EU, this holds especially true for a precise definition of the economic and legal owner. While its general definition under Article 4 (20) provides valuable guidelines, unresolved details remain in particularly with regard to proprietary rights, factoring, buildings on third party land and leasing contracts.

C.3.4.2. Depreciation Base

The starting point for the determination of deductible depreciation expenses is to determine the depreciation base of the assets. Under the proposed Council Directive, assets qualifying for depreciation are initially measured at a full cost approach. According to Article 33 (1), the depreciation base compromises any costs directly related to the acquisition, construction or improvement of a fixed asset. In case the fixed asset is produced internally, the indirect costs incurred in the production is also to be included if they are not otherwise deductible. Subsidies directly linked to the acquisition, construction or improvement of fixed assets subject to depreciation are tax-exempt and are, therefore, excluded from the depreciation base (Article 11 (a)). As the support of research and development within the EU is one key aim of the Commission,[77] all costs relating to research and development are not capitalised but rather immediately deducted under the proposed Council Directive (Article 12).

In line with the proposed Council Directive, all considered countries require depreciable assets to be valued at historical costs at the time of purchase or production. In addition, the acquisition costs are determined by taking the purchase price and all directly attributable costs of purchase and installation into account. Likewise, most countries require or at least allow the full cost approach in determining production costs. As the discussion on the initial measurement of stock items and work-in-progress in subchapter C.3.3.2 has shown, there are indeed considerable differences in details. Yet, since most EU Member States as well as Switzerland and the US do not differentiate between the initial measurement of stock items and other assets we can refer to the detailed discussion in subchapter C.3.3.2. However, as the promotion of research and development activities has been one of the key aims of the proposed Council Directive we focus on the accounting for research and development costs in more detail in the following.

Research and Development Costs

Figure 31 provides an overview of the treatment of research and development costs in all considered countries. Although the line between research and development costs is hard to draw in practice, 13 of the 28 considered countries treat research and development costs differently. In doing so, almost all countries tie or refer tax accounting regulations for research and development costs to local GAAP or IAS/IFRS. Hence, the deduction of R&D costs often depends on the company's financial accounting policy.

In line with the proposed Council Directive a vast majority of countries under consideration charge all research costs immediately to expense. There is, however, a group of 7 countries – among them Belgium, Greece and the US – which grant an option to either capitalise or expense research costs immediately. Furthermore, capitalisation is mandatory in Bulgaria, Cyprus, Malta and Spain. Yet, in some countries (e.g. Luxembourg) research costs may only be capitalised if they are directly related to production.

---

[77] See explanatory memorandum of the proposed Council Directive.

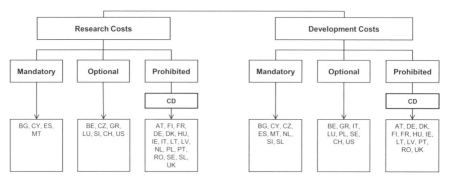

Figure 31: Capitalisation of Research and Development Costs

Bulgaria, Cyprus, the Czech Republic, Malta, the Netherlands, Slovakia, Slovenia and Spain require development costs to be capitalised after technical and commercial feasibility of the asset has been established. In contrast, all other countries prescribe or at least allow for an option to expense development costs immediately.

Improvement Cost

According to Article 35 improvement costs are to be depreciated in accordance with the rules applicable to the improved fixed asset as if they relate to a newly acquired fixed asset. In addition, Article 4 (18) defines improvement costs as any additional expenditure that materially increases the capacity of the asset, materially improves its functioning or represents more than 10% of the initial depreciation base of the asset. All other subsequent expenditure is to be recognised as an expense in the period in which it is incurred.

As displayed in Figure 32, improvement costs are generally capitalised in 26 of the 28 countries under consideration if certain conditions are met, e.g. the amount incurred is material or the costs of improvement provide benefits over a limited period of time. In contrast, improvement costs are, in general terms, expensed immediately in Belgium and Malta. However, it has to be kept in mind that some countries limit the capitalisation of improvement costs. For example, only if they exceed EUR 40,000 in the Czech Republic, improvement costs are treated as technical improvement and may be capitalised. Furthermore, some countries require that further benefits can be expected (e.g. Latvia), prolong the lifetime of the asset (e.g. Lithuania) or increase the production capacity (e.g. Spain).

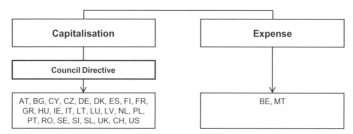

Figure 32: Treatment of Improvement Costs

As in the discussion on the initial measurement of the costs of stock and work-in-progress, it has to be emphasised that the definition of the depreciation base under Article 33 and the regulations on the depreciation of improvement costs under Article 35 must be seen as a first idea of what is to be measured as acquisition or production costs under the proposed Council Directive.[78] Comparing both regulations with national tax regulations, it becomes obvious that many details (e.g. a clear distinction between direct and indirect costs or an in-depth definition of individual cost components) are not provided.

Finally, it is important to note, that Article 44 provides special rules to deal with the differences between the proposed Council Directive and the national tax systems on transition to the CCCTB. As mentioned, assets and liabilities are recognised at their value according to the applicable national regulations immediately prior joining the system of the proposed CCCTB (Article 44). Consequently, there should be no liability to pay national taxes on joining the proposed CCCTB.

C.3.4.3. Low-Value Assets

Under the proposed Council Directive all tangible and acquired intangible assets securing income for more than 12 months are, in general terms, to be capitalised and depreciated (Article 4 (14) and Article 13). Yet, an important exemption applies to tangible and acquired intangible assets with acquisition costs of less than EUR 1,000 (so-called low-value assets) as costs incurred for those low-value assets are immediately expensed under the proposed Council Directive.

Figure 33 shows that acquisition costs for assets qualifying as low-value assets are immediately expensed in the year of purchase or in the period of acquisition in most of the considered countries. In detail, 21 of the 28 considered countries immediately expense the costs of low-value assets. While the maximum amount of low-value assets – ranging between EUR 350 in Bulgaria and EUR 3,000 in Sweden – is generally regulated by law, the taxpayer itself determines the value up to which assets are immediately expensed in Latvia and Lithuania. Only in Belgium, Ireland, Malta, Spain, the United Kingdom, Switzerland and the US all assets are, in general, capitalised and depreciated based on their useful life.

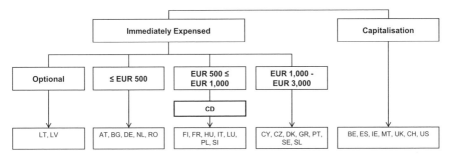

Figure 33: Treatment of Low-value Assets

---

[78] See also Kahle/Schulz (2011), p. 296.

C.3.4.4. *Individually Depreciable Assets*

According to Article 36 (1), individually depreciable assets include buildings, tangible assets with a useful life of over 15 years (e.g. long-life machinery and equipment) and intangible assets, all of which are discussed in detail in the following.

Buildings

Buildings are depreciated individually over their useful lives on a straight-line basis (Article 36 (1)). Furthermore, Article 36 sets the statutory useful life for buildings to 40 years. This useful life applies regardless of the type of building, i.e. a distinction between office and industrial buildings is not made. As exceptional depreciation is limited to non-depreciable assets (Article 41), it has to be noted that exceptional write-downs to the lower fair market value would not be allowed for any type of building under the proposed Council Directive.

As displayed in Figure 34, depreciation methods for industrial buildings[79] vary widely within the EU, Switzerland and the US. Yet, straight-line depreciation is the most common method. In this regard, 17 of the 28 considered countries are in line with the proposed Council Directive allowing acquisition or manufacturing costs of industrial buildings only to be depreciated in equal increments. In addition, Belgium, France, Lithuania and Switzerland provide for an option to either use the straight-line or the declining-balance method. In the Czech Republic, Malta, Poland and Slovakia taxpayers may choose between straight-line and accelerated depreciation. By contrast, Finland and Latvia provide only for the declining-balance method. Finally, in the United Kingdom, buildings do generally not qualify for depreciation. The same holds true for office buildings in Denmark, Ireland and Malta.

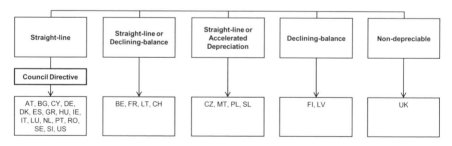

Figure 34: Depreciation of Industrial Buildings (Method)

---

[79] Please note that, in a first step, we only compare depreciation rules for industrial buildings. Yet, some countries under consideration (Belgium, Cyprus, the Czech Republic, Denmark, Finland, France, Greece, Ireland, Luxembourg, Malta, Portugal, Spain, Sweden and Switzerland) apply different depreciation rules for office and industrial buildings, we account for those differences by providing additional information on the depreciation of office buildings in Table 3.

With respect to the combination of two or more depreciation methods provided for in several countries, it is important to note that a switch-over to a different method is permitted only in Belgium and Switzerland. In contrast, once a particular method of depreciation has been chosen by the taxpayer in the Czech Republic, France, Lithuania, the Netherlands, Poland and Slovakia the method must be applied consistently over the entire life of the building; any kind of switch-over is prohibited.

In addition, differences between the proposed Council Directive and current tax accounting practice in the EU Member States, Switzerland and the US arise from different depreciation rates. In this respect, Table 3 provides an overview of the depreciation rates for industrial and office buildings in all considered countries.

Overall, depreciation periods under the straight-line method vary from 8 years in Lithuania to up to 100 years in the Netherlands, while the most frequent range is 20 to 50 years. Considerably higher depreciations rates are identified in those countries which also allow for the declining-balance method. A double declining-balance method is, for example, applicable in Belgium and Lithuania. In France the straight-line rate is increased by a multiplier of 2.25 whereas depreciation rates under the declining-balance method are fixed by law in Finland (7% / 4%), Latvia (10%) and Switzerland (8% / 4%).

Table 3: Depreciation of Industrial and Office Buildings (Rates)

Country	Straigth-line (Years)		Accelerated		Declining-balance	
	Industrial	Office	Industrial	Office	Industrial	Office
Council Directive	40	40	--	--	--	--
AT	33.33	33.33	--	--	--	--
BE	20	33.33	--	--	2 x SLR	2 x SLR
BG	min. 25	min. 25	--	--	--	--
CY	25	33	--	--	--	--
CZ	30	50	applicable[80]	applicable	--	--
DE	33	33	--	--	--	--
DK	25	prohibited	--	--	--	--
ES	33.33	50	--	--	--	--
FI	--	--	--	--	7 %	4%
FR	20	25	--	--	2.25 x SLR	2.25 x SLR
GR	12.5-20	20-33.33	--	--	--	--
HU	50	50	--	--	--	--
IE	25	prohibited	--	--	--	--
IT	33.33	33.33	--	--	--	--
LT	8-20	8-20	--	--	2 x SLR	2 x SLR
LU	20-25	20-50	--	--	--	--
LV	--,	--	--	--	10%	10%
MT	min. 50	prohibited	10% (initial allowance)	prohibited	--	--
NL	33.33-100 (fair value restriction)	33.33-100 (fair value restriction)	--	--	--	--
PL	10-40	10-40	1.2-1.4 x SLR[81]	1.2-1.4 x SLR	--	--
PT	20	50	--	--	--	--
RO	40-60	40-60	--	--	--	--
SE	25	50	--	--	--	--
SI	min. 33.33	min. 33.33	--	--	--	--
SL	20	20	applicable[82]	applicable	--	--
UK	prohibited	prohibited	--	--	--	--
CH	12.5-15	25-33.33	--	--	8%	4%
US	27.5-39	27.5-39	--	--	--	--

[80] If the accelerated method is used, the first year depreciation is set at a fraction of the input price and the appropriate coefficient stated in the rules on tax accounting. To determine the amount of the depreciation in subsequent years, the residual value must be doubled and divided by a specific coefficient. Accelerated depreciation is, in effect, a declining-balance method as it uses the same useful life as the straight-line method.

[81] The depreciation rates for straight-line depreciation are increased by a multiplier varying between 1.2 and 1.4 for buildings and constructions used in deteriorated or bad conditions.

[82] For the first year, the depreciation is computed by dividing the acquisition price of the asset by the coefficient for the first year of depreciation applicable to the depreciation category; in the second and following years, the residual tax book is first multiplied by two and then divided by the appropriate coefficient, which has been reduced by the number of years the depreciation has already been taken.

Machinery and Equipment (Long-life)

Tangible assets with a useful life of over 15 years belong to the group of individually depreciable assets under the proposed Council Directive (Article 36 (1)). Consequently, the same principles underlying the depreciation of buildings apply to long-life machinery and equipment: Tangible assets with a useful life of over 15 years are depreciated on a straight-line basis over their useful life which is set to 15 years. Exceptional write-downs to the lower fair market value are prohibited.

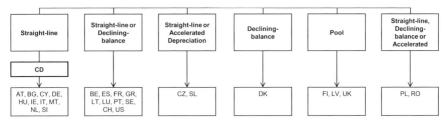

Figure 35: Depreciation of Long-life Machinery and Equipment (Method)

Figure 35 provides an overview of the methods of depreciation of long-life machinery and equipment in all countries under consideration. Almost all countries are in line with the proposed Council Directive and require companies to depreciate each asset separately on an individual basis. In doing so, it is common tax practice in the EU to prescribe – or at least allow for – straight-line depreciation. In detail, in 10 EU Member States long-life machinery and equipment may only be depreciated on a straight-line basis whereas companies in 10 of the 28 considered countries may either use the straight-line or the declining-balance method.[83] Moreover, taxpayers in the Czech Republic and Slovakia may choose between straight-line and accelerated depreciation. Even more generous, Poland and Romania apply all three methods of depreciation for long-life machinery and equipment. By contrast, Denmark strictly prescribes the declining-balance method. Finally, Finland, Latvia and the United Kingdom apply pool depreciation, which allows the addition of the depreciable bases of all long-life tangible assets and the calculation of the depreciation charge as an overall figure. For Latvia, it has to be noted that tangible assets are grouped into several pools to which different depreciation rates are applied. In contrast, Finland and the United Kingdom recognise only one pool of long-life tangible assets.

Similar to the treatment of buildings, some countries allow companies to switch over to another depreciation method, thereby allowing taxpayers to optimise their tax base. Subject to certain conditions, this holds true for Belgium, Luxembourg, Romania, Sweden, Switzerland and the US. In all other countries, one method must be applied consistently over the entire life of the tangible asset.

---

[83] Please note that this choice is only available for selected industry sectors in Greece.

Table 4: Depreciation of Long-life Machinery and Equipment (Rates)

Country	Straight-line (Years)	Accelerated	Declining-balance	Pool
Council Directive	15	--	--	--
AT	3-16.67	--	--	--
BE	3-10	--	2 x SLR	--
BG	25	--	--	--
CY	12.5-16.7	--	--	--
CZ	10	applicable	--	--
DE	3-16.67	--	--	--
DK	--	--	21%	--
ES	4-12.5	--	1.5-2.5 x SLR	--
FI	--	--	--	25%
FR	3-20	--	1.25-2.25 x SLR	--
GR	3.33-33.33	--	3 x SLR	--
HU	2-7	--	--	--
IE	8	--	--	--
IT	2.5-14	--	--	--
LT	3-8	--	2 x SLR	--
LU	5-15	--	max. 3 x SLR (limited to 30%)	--
LV	--	--	--	15-40%
MT	4-16.67	--	--	--
NL	min. 5	--	--	--
PL	7-10	1.2-2 x SLR	2 x SLR	--
PT	3-20	--	1.5-2.5 x SLR	--
RO	useful life	50% (initial allowance)	1.5-2.5 x SLR	--
SE	5	--	max. 30%	--
SI	3-10	--	--	--
SL	4-12	applicable	--	--
UK	--	--	--	10%
CH	4.44-13.33	--	15-45%	--
US	10-25	--	1.5-2 x SLR	--

Table 4 displays the depreciation rates applicable for long-life machinery and equipment in the EU Member States, Switzerland and the US. Overall, there is a remarkable dispersion of rates in the countries under consideration. In short, straight-line depreciation periods range from 2 years in Hungary up to 33.33 years in Greece. Yet, as the specific ranges are applicable for a number of different tangible assets, a general cross-country comparison in this area is difficult and might provide misleading results. In addition, one has to keep in mind that only Bulgaria, Cyprus, the Czech Republic, Denmark, Poland, Slovenia, the United Kingdom and the US explicitly differentiate between long-life and short-life machinery and equipment. In all other countries, the depreciation rates for long-life machinery and equipment are rather at the upper end of the range provided in Table 4.

Intangibles

Intangible assets can be internally developed or externally acquired. While the costs for internally developed intangibles would principally be expensed as incurred under the proposed Council Directive, externally acquired intangibles are considered as fixed assets subject to individual depreciation (Article 4 (14) and Article 36 (1)). Consequently, depreciation of acquired intangibles under the proposed Council Directive follows in principal the treatment of fixed tangible assets and buildings. The depreciation period is the useful life defined as the period for which the intangible enjoys legal protection or for which the right is granted. If this period cannot be determined, intangibles are depreciated over a period of 15 years.

a. Internally Developed Intangibles

One key aim of the proposed Council Directive is to support research and development within the EU.[84] Consequently, all costs relating to research and development are immediately expensed (Article 12) and internally developed intangibles do not qualify for capitalisation and depreciation.

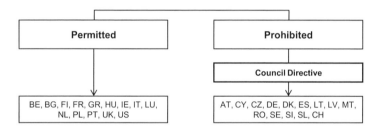

Figure 36: Capitalisation of Internally Developed Intangibles

As displayed in Figure 36, 14 of the 28 countries under consideration are in line with the proposed Council Directive and prohibit the capitalisation of costs for internally developed intangible assets. In these countries, intangibles must be acquired from third parties to qualify for capitalisation. Non-capitalisation may be justified with the uncertainty of intangibles relating to the value of the asset or as a matter of tax policy.[85] By contrast, internally developed intangible assets are capitalised and depreciated[86] in Belgium, Bulgaria, Finland, France, Greece, Hungary, Ireland,[87] Italy, Luxembourg, the Netherlands, Poland, Portugal, the United Kingdom and the US. Tax accounting rules in Greece, however, only allow the capitalisation of self-developed patents.

---

[84] See explanatory memorandum of the proposed Council Directive.

[85] See Schön (2004), p. 438.

[86] It should be noted that the same regulations applicable for acquired intangibles also prevail for internally developed assets. Therefore, we refer to the following subchapter.

[87] The aggregate amount of allowances and related interest expense that may be claimed for any accounting period is capped at 80% of the trading income of the relevant trade for that period.

b. Acquired Intangibles

In line with the proposed Council Directive, all countries under consideration require acquired intangible assets to be depreciated on an individual basis. As displayed in Figure 37, acquired intangibles are generally depreciated on a straight-line basis. Only Lithuania, Luxembourg, Sweden and Switzerland provide an option to depreciate acquired intangibles under the declining-balance method. In addition, taxpayers in Romania may opt for an accelerated depreciation scheme for patents only. It should be noted that the same regulations that apply to acquired intangibles also prevail for internally developed assets in Belgium, Bulgaria, Finland, France, Greece, Hungary, Ireland,[88] Italy, Luxembourg, the Netherlands, Poland, Portugal, the United Kingdom and the US.

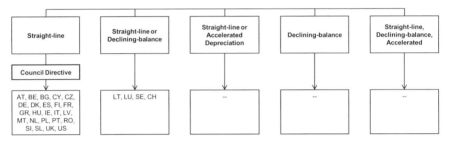

Figure 37: Depreciation of Acquired Intangibles (Method)

As a general assessment of the period over which acquired intangibles may be available for use is not without its problems, the vast majority of countries under consideration do not specify depreciation rates for acquired intangibles, but rather require acquired intangibles to be depreciated over their useful life (Table 5). By contrast, acquired intangibles may be depreciated over a statutory fixed period in Denmark (7 years), Finland (10 years), Latvia (5 years), Sweden (5 years) and the United Kingdom (25 years).[89] Other countries, e.g. Bulgaria, the Czech Republic or Italy, provide specific depreciation periods for different classes of intangible assets. The periods range from 1.5 years in the Czech Republic (audio – visual works) to 18 years for trademarks in Italy. In this respect, it has again to be noted that the specific ranges are given for a number of different intangible assets, therefore making general cross-country comparisons difficult.

---

[88] The aggregate amount of allowances and related interest expense that may be claimed for any accounting period is capped at 80% of the trading income of the relevant trade for that period in Ireland.

[89] After April 1, 2002 intangible assets in the United Kingdom may be depreciated at a 4% fixed rate (CTA 2009 730). The election for the 4% straight line amortisation is irrevocable and must be made in writing within two years of the end of the accounting period in which the asset is acquired or created by the company. Alternatively, the deductions for corporation tax purposes follow the accounts provided they are prepared in accordance with local GAAP.

Table 5: Depreciation of Acquired Intangibles (Rates)

Country	Straight-line (Years)	Accelerated	Declining-balance	Goodwill (Years)
Council Directive	legal protection / 15	--	--	15
AT	useful life	--	--	15
BE	min. 5 / 3 (R&D)	--	--	5-10
BG	2-6.67	--	--	prohibited
CY	useful-life (period of legal protection)	--	--	--
CZ	1.5-6	--	--	15
DE	useful life	--	--	15
DK	7[90]	--	--	7
ES	useful life (max. 10 years)	--	--	20
FI	10	--	--	10
FR	5-10	--	--	--
GR	useful life	--	--	max. 5
HU	useful life	--	--	--
IE	useful life	--	--	prohibited
IT	2-18	--	--	10-18
LT	3 or 4	--	2 x SLR	15
LU	useful life	--	max. 3 x SLR (limited to 30%)	10
LV	5[91]	--	--	prohibited
MT	useful life	--	--	prohibited
NL	min. 5	--	--	min. 10
PL	2-5	--	--	min. 5
PT	useful life	--	--	prohibited
RO	useful life[92]	--	--	prohibited
SE	5	--	max. 30%	5 (or max. 30%)
SI	min. 10	--	--	--
SL	useful life	--	--	7
UK	25	--	--	25
CH	useful life	--	40%	40% (5)
US	useful life	--	--	15

---

[90] Please note that the acquisition cost of patents and acquired know-how may be deducted in the year of acquisition if such rights are acquired in connection with the purchaser's business.

[91] Please note that for taxable periods from 2009 to 2013, the cost of developing patents or trademarks is multiplied by 1.5 for the purposes of tax depreciation.

[92] Please note that patents may be subject to accelerated depreciation on a reduced balance-method (33.33%)

c. Acquired Goodwill

In line with the proposed Council Directive, goodwill that is internally generated should not be recognised in all countries under consideration. By contrast, all considered countries require acquired goodwill to be capitalised. As displayed in Table 5, acquired goodwill does, however, not qualify for any form of depreciation in Bulgaria, Ireland, Italy, Latvia, Malta, Portugal and Romania. Rather, acquired goodwill reduces taxable income only upon disposal. Furthermore, Cyprus, France, Hungary and Slovenia follow a strict impairment-only approach, i.e. the costs are not amortised on an annual basis but goodwill should be tested for impairment annually.

Acquired goodwill may be depreciated in all other countries; however, there are remarkable differences between the methods and periods for depreciation (Table 5). In addition, only Denmark, Finland, Sweden and the United Kingdom apply the same methods and rates as for other intangible assets. In all other countries, national tax regulations provide for specific definitions and specifications of the length of the useful life. In doing so, acquired goodwill is to be depreciated on a straight-line basis in the vast majority of countries under consideration. Only Sweden and Switzerland also provide for the declining-balance method. Furthermore, as displayed in Table 5, the depreciation periods applicable for acquired goodwill generally tends to be higher than those for other intangible assets. The most frequent depreciation period – in line with the proposed Council Directive – is 15 years (in Austria, the Czech Republic, Germany, Lithuania and the US).

Even though acquired goodwill represents a substantial value for many companies, it remains at least questionable how acquired goodwill is treated under the proposed Council Directive. In principal, acquired goodwill meets the definition of fixed assets under Article 4 (14) (acquired for value, independently valued and securing income for more than 12 months) and should – from our perspective – qualify for individual depreciation over a period of 15 years under Article 36 (1). Nevertheless, without a clear determination of what is to be treated as an intangible asset under the proposed Council Directive, non-uniform interpretation among EU Member States is likely to occur. Not only in this respect does a suitable definition and classification of intangible assets that qualify for individual depreciation still have to be found by the Commission.

C.3.4.5. Asset Pool

According to Article 39 (1), fixed assets other than buildings, long-life tangible assets and intangible assets are to be depreciated under the pool method at an annual rate of 25% of the depreciation base. Article 39 (2) defines the depreciation base of the asset pool at the end of the tax year. Accordingly, the depreciation base amount to the pool value for tax purposes at the end of the previous year, adjusted for assets entering (which shall be added) and leaving (which shall be deducted) the pool during the current year. Adjustments are also to be made for construction or improvement costs of assets and any compensation received for the loss or destruction of pool assets. If the balance in the asset pool at the end of any year is negative, the negative balance is to be added back to the tax base to adjust the asset pool, i.e. the depreciation base, to zero (Article 39 (3)). Since short-life machinery and equipment is depreciated setting up a single asset pool, the proposed pool method eliminates many administrative issues that occur when each asset is treated on an individual basis, e.g. the classification of asset or the individual allocation at acquisition. Hence, the prescribed pool method seems much simpler to administer for both the taxpayer and for the tax authorities.

The economic implications of the pool method compared to individual depreciation on a straight-line basis obviously depend on the actual lifetime of the assets entering the pool. Overall, some assets entering the asset pool will have a longer economic life and some a shorter economic life than the one reflected by the standard depreciation rate of 25%. As displayed in Table 6 the differences between the applicable depreciation rate under the pool method and individual depreciation on a straight-line basis vary considerably with the lifetime of the assets.

Table 6: Comparison of Depreciation Rates under Straight-line and Pool Depreciation

Useful Life of Asset	2	3	4	10	15
Straight-line Depreciation Rate in %	50.00	33.33	25.00	10.00	6.67
Pool Depreciation Rate (Article 39 (1)) in %	25.00	25.00	25.00	25.00	25.00

While the differences between the two methods are smaller for short-term machinery and equipment (e.g. computers, tools etc.), significant differences arise for fixed assets with a useful life at the upper range of the asset pool (heavy machinery, trucks etc.). Yet, it shall be noted that there is an offsetting mechanism inherent in a pooling approach. Nevertheless, the economic implication of the implementation of an asset pool may – depending on the asset structure – differ considerably across companies or industry segments.

Finally it is important to note, that – in line with the general rollover relief for individually depreciable fixed assets (Article 38)[93] – the pool method ensures that the taxation of gains on the disposal of assets is spread over the lifetime of replacement assets, thereby providing incentives to reinvest. Gains on the disposal of pooled assets are only taxed once the asset pool becomes negative. In this respect, the simplified example provided for in Table 7 may illustrate the implications of this mechanism.

---

[93] For details, see subchapter C.3.1.3.

Table 7: Capital Gains Taxation and Pool Depreciation

	Case 1	Case 2	Case 3
Opening Pool Balance	10,000	10,000	10,000
Add			
Costs of Replacement Asset Acquired	20,000	20,000	20,000
Deduct			
Proceeds from Disposal of Pooled Asset	15,000	25,000	35,000
Add-back (Article 39 (3))	--	--	5,000
Closing Pool Balance	15,000	5,000	0
Other Deductible Expenses / Depreciation (25%)	3,750	1,250	--
Taxable Gain	--	--	5,000

Consider an asset pool with an opening balance amounting to EUR 10,000. Now suppose the disposal of a pooled asset for EUR 15,000 (Case 1), EUR 25,000 (Case 2) and EUR 35,000 (Case 3) respectively and the subsequent acquisition of a replacement asset for EUR 20,000. According to Article 11 all proceeds from the disposal of pooled assets are exempt from corporate income tax. Yet, the proceeds from the disposal of pooled assets reduce the value of the pool (Article 39 (2)). At the same time, the pool balance is, however, increased by the subsequent acquisition of any (replacement) asset. As a result, any gain on disposal is deducted from the depreciation base of the pool, rather than immediately taxed. However, one has to keep in mind, that the taxation is only postponed to subsequent years as the reduction of the depreciation base results in lower depreciation over time. In addition, if the disposal results in a negative pool balance (Case 3), the gain on disposal is added to the depreciation base and immediately taxed to the extent the proceeds exceed the remaining balance of the pool (Article 39 (3)).

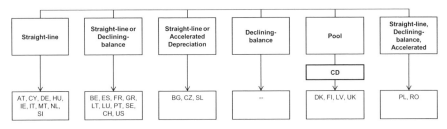

Figure 38: Depreciation of Short-life Machinery and Equipment (Method)

In contrast to the proposed Council Directive, almost all of the considered countries require companies to depreciate each tangible asset separately on an individual basis (Figure 38). Again, the straight-line and the declining-balance method are the two most common methods in the considered countries. In addition, accelerated depreciation schemes exist in Bulgaria, the Czech Republic, Poland, Romania and

Slovakia. In line with the proposed Council Directive, only in Denmark, Finland, Latvia and the United Kingdom qualifying expenditures are pooled for the purpose of computing tax depreciation.[94]

Table 8: Depreciation of Short-life Machinery and Equipment (Rates)

Country	Straight-line (Years)	Accelerated	Declining-balance	Pool
Council Directive	--	--	--	25%
AT	3-16.67	--	--	--
BE	3-10	--	2 x SLR	--
BG	2-10	50%	--	--
CY	2-10	--	--	--
CZ	3-10	applicable	--	--
DE	3-16.67	--	--	--
DK	--	--	--	25%
ES	4-12.5	--	1.5-2.5 x SLR	--
FI	--	--	--	25%
FR	3-20	--	1.25-2.25 x SLR	--
GR	3.33-33.33	--	3 x SLR	--
HU	2-7	--	--	--
IE	8	--	--	--
IT	2.5-14	--	--	--
LT	3-8	--	2 x SLR	--
LU	5-15	--	max. 3 x SLR (limited to 30%)	--
LV	--	--	--	20-70%
MT	4-16.67	--	--	--
NL	min. 5	--	--	--
PL	3.33-10	1.2-2 x SLR	2 x SLR	--
PT	3-20	--	1.5-2.5 x SLR	--
RO	useful life	50% (initial allowance)	1.5-2.5 x SLR	--
SE	5	--	max. 30%	--
SI	2-5	--	--	--
SL	4-12	applicable	--	--
UK	--	--	--	20%
CH	4.44-13.33	--	15-45%	--
US	3-7	--	2 x SLR	--

Similar to the treatment of long-life assets, some Member States allow companies to switch depreciation methods, thereby allowing taxpayers to reduce their tax base. Again, conditional upon meeting certain requirements, this is true for Belgium, Luxembourg, Romania, Sweden, Switzerland and the US. In all other countries, one method must be applied consistently over the entire life of the tangible assets.

---

[94] The US does not apply pool depreciation in a proper sense. Instead of individual depreciation, assets are merely divided into at least two depreciation classes. The asset classes are depreciated using the declining-balance method. The depreciation base is the acquisition costs and a switch-over to straight-line depreciation is allowed.

Once more, a general cross-country comparison of depreciation periods and rates is difficult. In addition, one has to keep in mind that only Bulgaria, Cyprus, the Czech Republic, Denmark, Poland, Slovenia, the United Kingdom and the US explicitly differentiate between long-life and short-life machinery and equipment. Nevertheless, some general comparative conclusions on the treatment of short-life machinery and equipment are possible (Table 8). First, there is considerable variation concerning the depreciation periods for different assets under the straight-line method. Even for countries distinguishing between short-life and long-life assets, the straight-line periods range from 2 years (e.g. in Bulgaria and Slovenia) up to 10 years (e.g. in Cyprus and the Czech Republic). Second, and more important, the proposed Council Directive tends to be more generous than the depreciation regulations in most countries under consideration with respect to short-life tangible assets. Yet, the countries that also apply a pool-system provide comparably high depreciation rates. In this respect, Denmark and Finland are in line with the proposed Council Directive applying the same depreciation rate of 25%, whereas the United Kingdom (20%) provides for a lower rate in the single plant and machinery pool. By contrast, several asset pools for short-life tangible assets exist in Latvia (20% – 70%).

To sum up, the regular depreciation regulation governed by Article 32 – 39 of the proposed Council Directive follow a distinct and internationally prevailing standard that is not new to the EU, Switzerland and the US. Overall, regulations are mainly similar in key principles, but different in details; e.g. with respect to the depreciation methods and rates. Yet, open questions remain regarding the following: The proposed Council Directive contains no specific information regarding the determination of the useful life of assets. Whether the determination of the useful life of assets is to be based on the economical or technical lifetime of the assets, still needs to be defined. In order to unambiguously determine whether the individual or the pool depreciation method shall be applicable, clarification is also required concerning the determination of the useful life of machinery and equipment, e.g. by more precise description of different categories of fixed assets as designated by Article 42.

At this point, it should also be emphasised that the proposed Council Directive provides detailed rules to account for differences in depreciation regulations between the proposed Council Directive and national tax accounting on transition to the CCCTB. According to Article 45 (1), all fixed asset entering the CCCTB system shall be depreciated according to the regulation provided for under the proposed Council Directive (Article 31 – Article 42). Notwithstanding this general rule, the transitional rules as displayed in Table 9 shall apply (Article 45 (2)). Most important, fixed assets that are included in an asset pool under national tax accounting shall always enter the asset pool, even if they would be individually depreciated under the proposed Council Directive. Consequently, the tax book value under the national tax accounting regulations is to be added to the depreciation base of the single asset pool. By contrast, fixed assets that are individually depreciable under national tax accounting but not under the proposed Council Directive shall enter the asset pool.

Table 9: Transitional Rules on Joining the Proposed CCCTB (Depreciation)

Applicable Depreciation Method (Article 45 (2))	Depreciation under National Tax Accounting	Depreciation under the Proposed Council Directive
Individual Depreciation / Second-Hand Depreciation (Article 36 (2))	Individual Depreciation	Individual Depreciation
Asset Pool (Article 39)	Individual Depreciation	Asset Pool
Asset Pool (Article 39)	Asset Pool	Individual Depreciation / Asset Pool

With respect to individual depreciable assets, Article 36 (2) stipulates that upon joining the CCCTB system, the useful lifetime applies as if all assets are new, unless the taxpayer can demonstrate that the estimated remaining useful life of the asset is shorter. For example, a building shall be depreciated over 40 years unless the taxpayer demonstrates that the estimated remaining useful life of the building is shorter than 40 years. In this regard, taxpayers may be confronted with substantial longer depreciation periods when entering the CCCTB. It should also be noted, that it remains unclear how the taxpayer may provide evidence on the abbreviated remaining useful life under the proposed Council Directive.

C.3.4.6. Assets not subject to Depreciation

According to Article 40 fixed tangible assets not subject to wear and tear and obsolescence (e.g. land and financial assets) are not subject to regular depreciation under the proposed Council Directive. In this respect, all countries under consideration are in line with the proposed Council Directive. It is common tax practice in all EU Member States, Switzerland and the US that decreases in value of land and financial assets are not accounted for on a basis of regular but rather by exceptional depreciation. Please note that fixed assets that are not depreciable under national tax law but are depreciable under rules of the proposed Council Directive shall be depreciated under the regulations of Articles 32 – 42 (Article 45 (2)).

C.3.4.7. Exceptional Depreciation

In contrast to assets subject to regular depreciation, Article 41 of the proposed Council Directive allows exceptional depreciation for non-depreciable assets which have permanently decreased in value and are taxed upon disposal. If the value of non-depreciable assets subsequently increases, an amount equivalent to the increase is to be added to the tax base. Yet, the write-up is limited to the amount previously deducted.

As displayed in Figure 39, exceptional depreciation for assets which have permanently decreased in value is – irrespective of whether the underlying asset is depreciated on a regular basis or not – permitted in Austria, Finland, France,[95] Germany, Hungary, Luxembourg, the Netherlands and Spain. In addition, Sweden deviates from the proposed Council Directive allowing extraordinary write-downs only for assets subject to regular depreciation.[96] In contrast, extraordinary depreciation is limited to non-depreciable assets in Belgium, the Czech Republic and Slovenia.[97] The majority of countries under consideration, however, strictly prohibits or at least neutralises the tax effect of extraordinary write-downs. In this respect, only the United Kingdom, Switzerland and the US provide for certain exceptions, e.g. extraordinary depreciation of intangible assets in the United Kingdom.

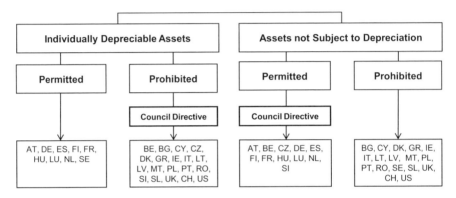

Figure 39: Exceptional Depreciation

Finally, in line with the proposed Council Directive, subsequent increases in value may be taxed in most considered countries allowing for extraordinary write-down. Nevertheless, the write-up may not exceed historical acquisition or production costs in all countries under consideration. By contrast, write-ups of assets subject to extraordinary depreciation are generally prohibited in Finland and Sweden.

Overall, with regard to extraordinary depreciation, the proposed Council Directive prescribes more restrictive rules compared to many other countries under consideration. From a mere economic perspective, there is no justification to limit exceptional depreciation to non-depreciable assets as it places excessive constraints on the deduction of losses. Furthermore, in practice, the limitation is likely to force taxpayers to dispose depreciable assets, but to retain a beneficial interest in them in order to benefit immediately from loss relief. Finally, as there is a lack of clarity as to what constitutes a permanent decrease in value of non-depreciable assets, further clarification in this respect is also necessary.

---

[95] Please note that exceptional depreciation is not allowed for buildings in France.
[96] As for France, depreciation is not allowed for buildings in Sweden.
[97] Please note that intangible assets also qualify for extraordinary depreciation in Slovenia.

C.3.5. Non-Deductible Expenses[98]

Important differences between the proposed Council Directive and the national tax regulations may arise in distinguishing between productive / deductible expenses and private expenses, which are non-deductible.[99] The proposed Council Directive provides a comprehensive list of non-deductible expenses in Article 14 (1), including, for example, distributed profits, corporate income tax or fines and penalties. In addition, Article 15 governs that those benefits granted to controlling shareholders, their descendants or associated enterprises[100] are treated as non-deductible to the extent that such benefits would not be granted to an independent third party. In the following, these non-deductible expenses are classified into three different categories and discussed in more detail in the cross-country setting. Finally, the deduction of interest payments and thin-capitalisation rules are addressed.

C.3.5.1. Categories of Expenses

Category 1: Profit Distributions, Repayments and Other Benefits of Shareholders

The fist category of non-deductible expenses considered here includes profit distributions and repayments of debt (Article 14 (1) (a)). Moreover, Article 15, which is essentially a codification of the arm's length principle, provides, in short, that expenses incurred for the benefits of shareholders are not deductible to the extent that such benefits would not be granted to an independent third party. Yet, as the specific disallowance of those expenses seems to refer to commonly accepted principles of accounting and taxation, it serves as an important example for the general necessity of the proposed Council Directive to provide rules that cover all aspects of determining the common tax base in order to ensure uniform application and treatment across all Member States.

---

[98] Please note that corporations in Estonia are only subject to a flat-rate tax on distributed profits, including transactions that are considered hidden profit distributions. The latter includes costs not related to the business (e.g. penalties, bribes or membership fees), certain gifts and donations, certain entertainment expenses and fringe benefits as well as benefits to shareholders.

[99] See also Garcia (2008), p. 347.

[100] For a detailed definition of the terms controlling shareholder and associated enterprise, please refer to Article 15 and Article 78 of the proposed Council Directive.

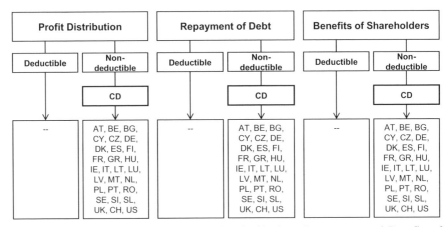

Figure 40: Non-Deductible Expenses: Profit Distributions, Repayments and Benefits of Shareholders

As displayed in Figure 40, the non-deductibility of profit distributions and repayments of debt is commonly accepted in all countries under consideration. In detail, there is no single country in the European Union or beyond that allows a deduction of profit distributions and repayments of debt. The same holds true for expenditures incurred for the benefits of shareholders that do not meet the criteria of the arm's length principle.

Category 2: Taxes

According to Article 14 (1) (d) corporate taxes are to be treated as non-deductible expenses under the proposed Council Directive. Furthermore, Article 14 (1) (j) prohibits the deduction of local business taxes, real estate taxes and most other taxes levied on income or capital by the Member States.[101] Although these regulations may at first glance oppose the main principle of Article 12, which states that taxes – as expenses to obtain and secure income – are generally deductible, the treatment of local taxes as non-deductible expenses has to be seen in the overall context of the CCCTB. Rather than allowing all local taxes to be deducted from the (consolidated) tax base, local taxes might be deducted after the common (consolidated) tax base has been allocated to the respective Member States provided that national tax law allows such deductions. As local taxes are therefore deducted from each individual Member State's share of the consolidated tax base, an undesired impact on the apportionment of the CCCTB for Member States that do not levy local taxes is prohibited.

---

[101] Please see Annex III of the proposed Council Directive for a list of all non-deductible taxes for each Member State.

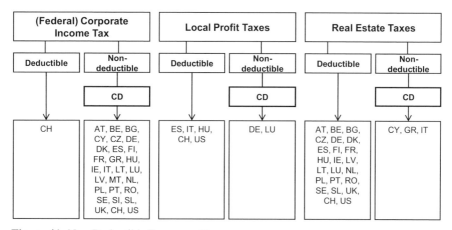

Figure 41: Non-Deductible Expenses: Taxes

At this point it should also be emphasised that similar issues are raised in respect to social security contributions, which are generally deductible from the tax base under the proposed Council Directive. Since the funding of social security systems differs considerably across EU Member States[102], undesired implications for the consolidation and sharing mechanism may arise. While the deductibility of social security contributions put those Member States that fund their social security systems by general tax revenue at a disadvantage, other Member States that finance their systems by tax deductible social security contributions would obviously benefit and – at least to some extent – free ride on the common tax base.[103] How this problem will be solved still remains a controversial issue and makes another good case for the European Commission to consider the strategy of introducing the CCCTB in a two-step approach.

As displayed in Figure 41, (federal) corporate income taxes are – in line with the proposed Council Directive – treated as non-deductible expenses in all considered countries except Switzerland.[104] In contrast, the vast majority of countries under consideration allow real estate taxes to be deducted from the corporate income tax base. Yet, while there is no real estate tax imposed in Malta and Slovenia, such deductions are prohibited in Cyprus, Greece[105] and Italy. At the same time, local profit taxes are, however, deductible in Italy.[106] The same holds true for Hungary, Spain, Switzerland and the US. As local profit taxes are not imposed in

---

[102] See European Commission (2008) and, for an overview of social security contributions in Europe Elschner (2008).

[103] See Spengel/Wendt (2008) and Fuest (2008), p. 725.

[104] In Switzerland, the federal direct tax is levied at a flat rate of 8.5%. This corresponds to an effective rate of 7.83% when the deductibility of the tax from its own tax base is taken into consideration.

[105] Please note that the local real estate duty, however, is, deductible for income tax purposes in Greece.

[106] Please note that only 10% of the regional tax on productive activities (IRAP) is deductible in Italy.

all other considered countries, municipal business taxes are treated as non-deductible expenses only in Germany and Luxembourg.

Category 3: Costs Incurred for Exempt Income, Entertainment Costs and Fines

The third category includes expenses that are classified as (partially) non-deductible expenses, even though they may be incurred with a view to obtain or secure business income. In detail, Article 14 (1) (e) and (f) define bribes as well as fines and penalties payable to a public authority for breach of legislation as non-deductible expense. In addition, only 50% of entertainment costs (Article 14 (1) (b)) and monetary gifts and donations other than those to charitable bodies (Article 14 (1) (h)) are classified as non-deductible. Most important, however, Article 14 (1) (g) provides that those costs incurred by a company for the purpose of deriving tax exempt income (e.g. received profit distributions, proceeds from the disposal of shares[107]) are non-deductible under the proposed Council Directive. Such costs are fixed at a flat rate of 5% of the tax-exempt income unless the taxpayer is able to demonstrate that lower costs have been incurred.

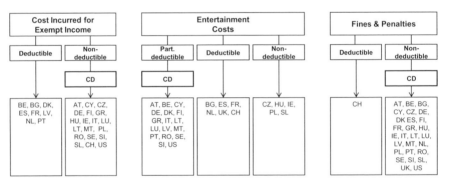

Figure 42: Non-Deductible Expenses: Costs Incurred for Exempt Income, Entertainment Costs and Fines

As summarised in Figure 42, the vast majority of countries under consideration are in line with the proposed Council Directive and (partially) prohibit the deduction of fines and penalties, entertainment costs or bribes. In detail, fines and penalties are not deductible in all considered countries except Switzerland. In addition, while the majority of countries (22) at least partially prohibit the deduction of entertainment costs, Bulgaria, France, the Netherlands, Spain, the United Kingdom and Switzerland, in general, treat entertainment costs as fully deductible business expenses. Finally, costs directly related to tax exempt income are not deductible in 19 of the 28 considered countries. By contrast, those expenses are generally deductible in Belgium, Bulgaria, Denmark, France, Latvia, the Netherlands, Portugal and Spain if they do not fall into the general category of non-deductible expenses. In the

---

[107] For details on tax exempt revenues, see subchapter C.3.2.

United Kingdom, however, the deductibility of expenses is determined on an individual basis. Hence, there is no specific rule which links costs to exempt income.

In summary, it has to be emphasised that Article 14 (1) provides a comprehensive and detailed list of expenses classified as non-deductible. Yet, it has to be kept in mind that the definition of certain terms (e.g. the exact definition of entertainment costs or bribes) might be understood differently in each Member State.[108] Thus, further clarification of these terms seems to be necessary in order to guarantee uniform treatment in all Member States.

C.3.5.2. Interest Expenses

As a general rule, all interest paid by a company with a view of obtaining or securing income is deductible from taxable income under the proposed Council Directive (Article 12). Yet, Article 81 limits the deductibility of interest payments under certain conditions. Accordingly, interest – as defined by Article 81 (2) – paid to an associated enterprise resident in a third country shall not be deductible where there is no agreement on the exchange of information and where one of the following conditions is met:

(1) The general statutory tax rate in the third country is lower than 40% of the average statutory corporate tax rate applicable in the Member States; or
(2) The associated enterprise is subject to a special tax regime which allows for a substantial lower level of taxation than that of the general regime.

By way of exception, such interest is still deductible under the escape clause of Article 81 (3). Accordingly, interest expenses are fully deductible if the amount of interest paid does not exceed the amount which would be stipulated between independent parties (arm's length principle).[109]

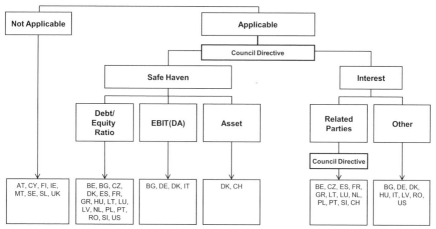

Figure 43: Thin-capitalisation Rules / Deductibility of Interest Expenses

---

[108] By contrast, Article 16 lays down the definition of charitable bodies to the last detail.
[109] For a more general discussion on thin-capitalisation rules in the context of the CCCTB, see Dourado/de la Feria (2008).

While it is far beyond the scope of this study to analyse and discuss the deductibility of interest expenses and thin-capitalisation rules applied in all considered countries in full detail, it is important to note that national practice regarding thin-capitalisation diverge widely across Member States.[110] As displayed in Figure 43, only 8 of the 28 considered countries do not apply specific thin-capitalisation rules, among them Austria,[111] Sweden and the United Kingdom.[112] By contrast, the vast majority of countries under consideration have implemented specific thin-capitalisation rules. Among those, there are significant differences regarding their specific design. Most important, while the thin-capitalisation or interest limitation rules in Bulgaria, Denmark, Germany, Hungary, Italy, Latvia, Romania and the US extend to related parties and third-party lenders, the majority of countries apply thin-capitalisation rules – in line with the proposed Council Directive – only to interest payable on debt owing to any related party.

In most of the considered countries a corporation is regarded as thinly-capitalised if debt exceeds certain prescribed debt to equity ratios. By contrast, the total debt of a company may not exceed the aggregate value of certain assets in Denmark and Switzerland. Moreover Bulgaria, Denmark, Germany and Italy apply so-called earnings-stripping rules, which limit the maximum interest deduction to certain EBIT(DA) thresholds. Yet, in line with the proposed Council Directive, almost all countries applying some form of thin-capitalisation rules provide the opportunity to prove that the transactions were at arm's length or provide for other escape clauses.

Finally, it is worth mentioning that Article 81 of the proposed Council Directive has been designed in the overall context of the CCCTB assuming consolidation and allocation of the common tax base across Member States. As shifting profits through interest payments between Member States would be eliminated within a CCCTB group, the regulations laid down in Article 81 are more or less relevant to associated enterprises resident in a third-country only. Considering the two-step harmonisation approach as outlined above, however, it seems at least questionable whether Member States are likely to follow the less restrictive thin-capitalisation rules of Article 81 under a CCTB or whether they continue to protect their national tax base by applying more restrictive national thin-capitalisation regulations.

---

[110] Please note that in practice and as highlighted above, thin-capitalisation rules are often highly complex and usually depend on various conditions. Therefore, the following must be seen as a rough overview of the regulations currently applied in the countries under consideration. For a more detailed overview see Dourado/de la Feria (2008) and Bohn (2010).

[111] Please note that courts have established certain guidelines which are used to determine whether a corporation is regarded thinly-capitalised.

[112] Please note that the thin-capitalisation rules are included in the transfer pricing legislation in the United Kingdom.

C.4. Loss Relief

Losses are incurred when deductible expenses and other deductible items exceed revenues in the tax year (Article 4 (10)). According to Article 43 (1) taxpayers that incur losses are able to deduct these losses in subsequent tax years, thereby reducing future taxable income. In other words, losses are eligible for carryforward indefinitely, but there is no carryback of losses to previous years under the proposed Council Directive. Moreover, as the proposed Council Directive generally does not distinguish between gains and losses as ordinary or capital[113], restrictions on the set-off of losses against profits within the same tax period do not apply. Furthermore, so-called minimum tax regulations, which limit the offset of losses to certain thresholds or guarantee a minimum tax payment even in case of losses, do not apply under the proposed Council Directive.

Even though losses may be carried forward indefinitely, loss carryforwards may be forfeited under the so-called loss trafficking rules (e.g. change-in-ownership rules and certain rules on reorganisations). Yet, such forfeiture of the loss carryforward does, in general, not apply under the proposed Council Directive. Rather, Article 71 provides that if one or more groups, or two or more members of a group, become as a result of a business reorganisation part of another group, any unrelieved losses is to be allocated to each of the members. If two or more principal taxpayers merge, any unrelieved loss of a group is to be allocated to its members and carried forward for future years.

C.4.1. Capital Losses

As a general rule losses may be offset against current profits in all countries under consideration. Yet, loss offset restrictions apply in those countries that distinguish between gains and losses as either ordinary or capital. While most countries under consideration do not allow for the deduction of losses corresponding to exempt capital gains (e.g. capital losses arising from the sale of shares), Cyprus, Ireland, Malta, the United Kingdom and the US, which all tax capital gains under a special relief, additionally limit the deductibility of any capital loss to future capital gains. For example, as capital gains are generally taxable as ordinary income, capital losses may also be offset against ordinary income for the current year in Germany. Only those capital losses arising from the sale of shares in companies – as the corresponding gains are tax exempt – are not deductible. In contrast, capital losses of companies in the US may be deducted only against capital gains. Any excess capital loss may only be carried back or forward and cannot be offset against ordinary income for the current year.

C.4.2. Ordinary Losses

As displayed in Figure 44 ordinary losses may be carried forward and set off against taxable income in all considered countries. Differences arise, however, with respect to the carryforward period. While 15 out of the 28 considered countries are

---

[113] For the discussion on capital gains see subchapter C.3.1.3.

in line with the proposed Council Directive and allow for an unlimited loss carry-forward, losses can be carried forward only for a certain period in Bulgaria, the Czech Republic, Finland, Greece, the Netherlands, Poland, Portugal, Romania, Slovakia, Spain, Switzerland[114] and the US. Here, the carryforward period varies between 4 years (e.g. Portugal) and 20 years in the US.

In contrast, losses are allowed to be carried back only in 6 of the 28 countries under consideration.[115] In France, Germany, Ireland (for trading losses) and the United Kingdom (for trading losses), losses may be carried back for one year prior to the year in which the losses incurred. In addition, Germany limits the absolute amount of the loss carryback to EUR 511,500. Yet, if a company ceases to carry on a trade, the loss carryback is increased to 3 years in the United Kingdom. The US restricts the loss carryback to 2 years. The longest carryback period of three year can be found in the Netherlands.[116] In addition, the Netherlands is the only consid-ered country that enforces a loss carryback if sufficient profits in previous tax years are available. In the other five countries, the carryback is optional.

Finally, it is important to note that Austria, France, Germany, Italy and Poland provide relative limitations of the loss carryforward (minimum tax regulations). In France and Germany, the basic amount is EUR 1,000,000. Exceeding losses may be set off against 60% of total taxable income above the basic amount, i.e. a minimum taxation of 40% of income applies. The other three countries do not apply a basic amount. In Austria and Italy[117], ordinary losses may be offset against future taxable income up to a limit of 75% and 80% of the taxable income, respectively. In Poland, only 50% of losses may be set off against profits each year.

---

[114] There is, in general, no carryback of losses allowed in Switzerland, except in Thurgau, where losses may be carried back for one year to be set off against profits.

[115] Please note that a loss carryback is generally prohibited in Hungary; however, companies involved in agriculture business may carry back losses to the two previous years.

[116] Please note that from 1 January 2007, losses sustained in the current fiscal year may be carried back only to the preceding year and forward for 9 years. For tax years 2009 to 2011 companies may opt for a loss carryback of 3 years. In such a case, the loss carryforward is restricted to 6 years.

[117] On 14 September, 2011, the Italian parliament approved the „austerity package", which also includes a new regime for tax losses. Losses derived in the first 3 years at the beginning of a business activity can be carried forward without time restrictions. The new regime applies to all losses incurred in the fiscal year 2011 for companies with a fiscal year that equals the calen-dar year.

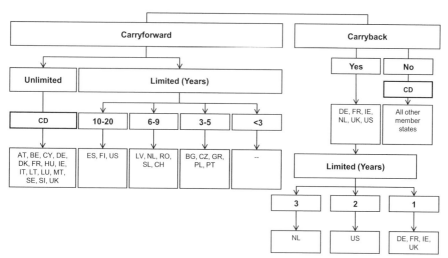

Figure 44: Loss Relief – Ordinary Losses

Regarding losses incurred prior joining the CCCTB, Article 48 provides that such losses remain available for loss relief under the proposed Council Directive if they could be carried forward under the applicable national tax regulations but had not yet been set off against taxable profits. Yet, those losses may be deducted from the common tax base only to the extent provided for under national tax accounting. As a result, any national limitations on the loss offset remain applicable to losses incurred prior joining the proposed CCCTB.

C.4.3. Forfeiture of Losses

As for our discussion on interest expenses and thin-capitalisation rules, it is far beyond the scope of this study to analyse and discuss the so-called loss trafficking rules applicable in all considered countries in full detail. However, some key features are displayed in Figure 45.

Most important, Figure 45 reveals that the vast majority of countries have established certain general loss trafficking regulations in order to prevent the sale or transfer of loss carryforwards to other companies. Yet, the country regulations differ widely with respect to the triggering event. While a substantial change in ownership of future profits results in a complete or prorated forfeiture of the loss carryforward in Belgium, Denmark, Finland, Germany, Latvia, the Netherlands, Sweden and the US, France focuses on a change of activity, i.e. a substantial modification of the operations carried out by the company. All other considered countries applying general loss trafficking rules more or less make use of a combination of both systems. Furthermore, it has to be noted that the loss carryforward remains available if certain conditions, e.g. the acquiring entity continues to carry out activities taken over for a specified period, are met in most of the countries under consideration (e.g. Finland, France, Italy, Lithuania and Portugal).

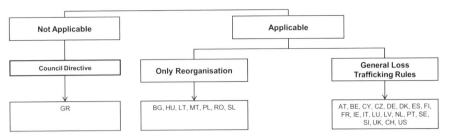

Figure 45: Forfeiture of Losses

By contrast, Bulgaria, Greece, Hungary, Lithuania, Malta, Poland, Romania and Slovakia are in line with the proposed Council Directive and apply no general loss trafficking regulations. Nevertheless, it has to be emphasised that in all countries under consideration countries expect Greece, loss carryforwards might be forfeited in case of mergers, divisions or similar restructuring operations.

D. Results

D.1. Summary of the Comparative Analyses

The proposal for a Council Directive on a CCCTB by the European Commission provides a carefully prepared and comprehensive framework for the determination of corporate taxable income. The comparison with the respective rules prevailing in the 27 EU Member States, Switzerland and the US illustrates that the proposed rules are, in general terms, in line with international standards and commonly accepted principles of tax accounting. The proposal provides detailed rules for a common corporate tax base (CCTB) that – from our perspective – can be expected to reach consensus in the EU. Nevertheless, individual Member States' current tax accounting practices obviously deviate from the proposed set of autonomous tax accounting rules under a CCTB in several ways. Table 10 provides an overview of these deviations and marks whether they constitute major or minor differences between the proposed Council Directive and current tax accounting practice. In this respect, not only the number of countries deviating from the proposed Council Directive is taken into consideration, but attention is also paid to the significance of differences.

Table 10: Summary of the Comparative Analyses: Proposed Council Directive on a CCCTB and Current Tax Accounting Practice in the 27 EU Member States, Switzerland and the US

Selected Issues of the Proposed Council Directive	Article	Deviation from Current Practice in the 27 EU Member States, Switzerland and the US	
		Major	Minor
Fundamental Concepts and General Principles			
Determination of the Tax Base: Starting Point			
Autonomous Tax Law	Explanatory Memorandum	✓	
Profit and Loss Account Approach	Article 10		✓
Basic Principles Underlying the Determination of the Tax Base			
Realisation Principle (Applied)	Article 9 (1)		✓
Item-by-Item Principle (Applied)	Article 9 (2)		✓
Consistency Requirement (Applied)	Article 9 (3)		✓
Anti-abuse Regulation (Applied)	Article 80		✓
Revenue			
Timing of Revenue			
General Principle (Accrual Principle)	Article 17 / 18		✓
Sales (Economic Ownership)	Article 17 / 18		✓
Profit Distributions (Dividend Resolution)	Article 17 / 18		✓
Interest (Accrual Basis)	Article 17 / 18		✓

Selected Issues of the Proposed Council Directive	Article	Deviation from Current Practice in the 27 EU Member States, Switzerland and the US	
		Major	Minor
Unrealised Revenue (Generally not Taxed)	Article 17 / 18		✓
Exceptions from the General Realisation Principle			
Financial Assets and Liabilities held for Trading (Taxed)	Article 23	✓	
Long-term Contracts (Percentage-of-Completion)	Article 24		✓
Controlled Foreign Company Rules (Applicable)	Article 82		✓
Taxation of Capital Gains			
General Principle (Taxable without Relief)	Article 4 (8)		✓
Replacement Assets (Rollover Relief)	Article 38	✓	
Exempt Revenue (Exempt Amount in Brackets)			
Profit Distributions (95%)	Article 11 (c)	✓	
Proceeds from Disposal of Shares (95%)	Article 11 (d)	✓	
Income of Foreign Permanent Establishments (100%)	Article 11 (e)		✓
Deductible Expenses			
General Principle (Obtaining / Securing Income)	Article 12		✓
Stocks and Work-in-Progress			
Initial Measurement (Direct Cost / Option to Include Indirect Cost)	Article 21 / 29 (2)		✓
Simplifying Valuation (FiFo, Weighted-average)	Article 29 (1)		✓
Subsequent Measurement (Lower of Cost and Market)	Article 29 (4)		✓
Bad Debt Receivables			
Specific Allowance (Permitted)	Article 27		✓
General Allowance (Permitted)	Article 27	✓	
Provisions			
Provisions for Liabilities			
Recognition (Permitted, Legal Obligation)	Article 25 (1)	✓	
Measurement	Article 25 (2)	✓	
Provisions for Contingent Losses (Permitted)	Article 25 (1)	✓	
Provision for Deferred Repair and Maintenance (Prohibited)	Article 25 (1)		✓
Warranty Provision (Permitted)	Article 25 (1)		✓
Pension Payments			
Direct Pension Scheme			
Recognition (Permitted)	Article 25 / 26	✓	
Measurement	Article 26	✓	
Indirect Pension Scheme (Permitted)	Article 12		✓

Selected Issues of the Proposed Council Directive	Article	Deviation from Current Practice in the 27 EU Member States, Switzerland and the US	
		Major	Minor
Other Deductible Items: Depreciation			
General Principles and Depreciation Base			
Entitlement to Depreciation (Economic Owner)	Article 34 / 4 (20)		✓
Timing of Depreciation (Full Year's Depreciation)	Article 37 (1)	✓	
Depreciation Base (Full Cost)	Article 33 (1)		✓
Research Costs (not Capitalised)	Article 12		✓
Development Costs (not Capitalised)	Article 12	✓	
Improvement Costs (Capitalised)	Article 35 / 4 (18)		✓
Regular Depreciation			
Low-value Assets (EUR 1,000; Immediately Expensed)	Article 13 / 4 (14)		✓
Internally Developed Intangibles (Immediately Expensed)	Article 36 (1) (c) / 4 (14)		✓
Individually Depreciable Assets (Buildings, Acquired Intangibles, Machinery and Equipment (Useful Life > 15 years))	Article 33 (1) / 36 (1)		✓
Asset Pool (Machinery and Equipment (Useful Life ≤ 15 years))	Article 39	✓	
Exceptional Depreciation			
Depreciable Assets (Prohibited)	Article 41		✓
Assets not Subject to Depreciation (Permitted)	Article 41	✓	
Non-deductible Expenses			
Group 1: Benefits Granted, Profit Distributions etc.	Article 14 (1) / 15		✓
Group 2: Tax Payments	Article 14 (1)	✓	
Group 3: Fines, Entertainment, Exempt Income	Article 14 (1)		✓
Group 4: Interest Expenses	Article 81	✓	
Losses			
Loss Carryforward (No Restrictions; Neither Amount nor Timing)	Article 43	✓	
Loss Carryback (Prohibited)	Article 43		✓
Loss Trafficking Rules (Not Applicable)	Article 71	✓	
Total: Summary Result		**19**	**33**

Since the rules for the determination of taxable income differ widely across the considered countries, it is a challenging task to compare the elements of the proposed Council Directive with current tax accounting practice in 29 different countries. Overall, the summary result of the 52 different elements of the proposed

Council Directive displayed in Table 10 reveals only minor differences. Obviously, the summary result is only a broad indicator. More detailed comparative conclusions about the key differences and similarities between the proposed Council Directive and current tax accounting practice are drawn in the following.

(1) The proposed Council Directive will introduce autonomous rules for computing and determining the corporate tax base and will not interfere with financial accounts. While the debate in preliminary stages has focused on the question whether and to what extent accounting principles as reflected in IFRS/IAS could be relied on, the proposed Council Directive cuts off all formal connections between financial and tax accounting. The lack of a formal link to IAS/IFRS or national GAAP constitutes one of the most fundamental differences between the proposed Council Directive and the national rules on tax accounting. The latter thoroughly refer to some extent to financial accounts as the starting point for the determination of taxable income.

(2) The general principles, in particular the realisation principle, underlying the determination of taxable income under the proposed Council Directive are in line with the general principles and fundamental criteria of tax accounting within the European Union, Switzerland and the US. Still, whether these general principles are sufficient enough to maintain consistency across all Member States and to operate as a tool for the interpretation of all relevant Articles provided by the proposed Council Directive remains to be seen. In particular, a clear legal concept and detailed definitions of legal terms still need to be established.[118]

(3) The determination of taxable income under the proposed Council Directive follows a profit and loss account approach. This is prevailing practice in the vast majority of countries under consideration. Yet, it is important to note, that both the profit and loss account and the balance sheet approach provide the same results (i.e. profit or loss) if any changes in the measurement of assets and liabilities are included in the profit and loss account. Consequently, and since financial accounting standards converge more and more across Europe, differences between the national tax systems cannot be found in the starting point of determining taxable income, but rather in the number and extent of prescribed deviations between financial and tax accounting.

(4) The recognition of revenue on an accrual basis and the more or less strict application of the realisation principle for tax purposes under the proposed Council Directive follow common and internationally accepted practice. Nevertheless, the interpretation and implementation of the realisation principle takes several forms in the countries under consideration. Most important, differences can be identified with respect to the extent of deviations from the general realisation principle, i.e. the taxation of unrealised revenues or the recognition of losses before realisation. In this regard, differences between the proposed Council Directive and current tax accounting practice arise prelimi-

---

[118] For a detailed discussion, see subchapter D.2.

narily from the tax effective revaluation of financial assets and liabilities held for trading.

(5) Like in the vast majority of the countries considered, capital gains are generally taxed as ordinary income without any relief under the proposed Council Directive. Major differences arise, however, with regard to the generous rollover relief for individually depreciable replacement assets provided by Article 38.

(6) Double taxation of foreign income, e.g. dividends, capital gains and income from foreign permanent establishments, is avoided by the strict application of the exemption method. Only if the level of foreign tax is too low, the exemption method is replaced by a tax credit. In this regard, major differences between the proposed Council Directive and prevailing tax practice arise with respect to the taxation of portfolio dividends and the disposal of portfolio shares. While exemption is granted irrespective of any minimum shareholding requirement under the proposed Council Directive, only revenues derived from substantial shareholdings qualify for preferential tax treatment in most countries under consideration.

(7) The fundamental concepts underlying the definition of deductible expenses under the proposed Council Directive are commonly accepted in all countries under consideration. While all costs incurred by the taxpayer with a view of obtaining or securing income qualify as deductible expenses, expenses made for private interest are not deductible. Nevertheless, the detailed implementation of this general principle takes various forms. In this regard, minor differences arise from the valuation of stock items and work-in-progress and from the treatment of bad debt receivables. By contrast, major differences exist with respect to the recognition and measurement of provisions.

(8) As the majority of countries under consideration generally prohibit tax deductions for provisions, the recognition and measurement of provisions form a major difference between the national tax accounting practice and the proposed Council Directive. The latter limits the recognition to matters relating to legal obligations. In this regard, tax accounting practice in those countries which generally allow provisions tends to be less restrictive than the proposed Council Directive. These countries also admit certain provisions for which the taxpayer is not legally obligated, e.g. provisions for deferred repair and maintenance costs. With regard to the measurement of provisions, the proposed Council Directive is consistent with international tax practice in essential principles. Differences mainly arise with respect to the consideration of future events and the discount rate. Nevertheless, the specification of a fixed discount rate by Article 25 is appropriate as it ensures an objective and uniform taxation and prevents opportunities for artificial tax planning. Finally, it is worth mentioning that it remains questionable whether or not contingent losses fall under the criteria of Article 25. In this regard, the vast majority of countries considered do not recognise contingent losses.

(9) Article 26 complements the general rules provided in Article 25 and sets out supplementary regulations for pension provisions. In short, actuarial techniques are to be used in order to determine the amount of provisions, which

shall be discounted by reference to the yearly average of Euribor for obligations with a maturity of 12 months. The application of a short-term discount
rate is questionable in this respect. Considering the long-term character of
pensions, a long-term discount rate seems more appropriate. Similar to the
discussion on general provisions, differences to the prevailing tax accounting
practice and open questions arise with respect to the detailed measurement of
pension provisions. Most important, in contrast to current tax practice, future
events, e.g. increases in salary, are taken into account when measuring pension provisions under the proposed Council Directive.

(10) The proposed Council Directive distinguishes between expenses that reduce
taxable income of the current period and capital expenditures, i.e. depreciation
expense. The latter are taken into account as other deductible items. Although
some important legal concepts still have to be defined, the proposed Council
Directive provides a comprehensive and objective framework in this regard.
The general principles, the determination of the depreciation base or the treatment of low-value assets are often similar to the essential regulations in all
countries under consideration and are expected to reach consensus among
Member States. Major differences arise, however, due to the combination of
the individual and the pool depreciation method under the proposed Council
Directive.

    a. Buildings, tangible assets with a useful life of more than 15 years (e.g.
long-life machinery and equipment) and intangible assets are depreciated
individually on a straight line basis over their fixed useful life. The international comparison reveals that individual depreciation is common practice
in the EU, Switzerland and the US. Differences between the proposed
Council Directive and prevailing tax practice arise, therefore, more or less
in details, e.g. concerning the depreciation methods and rates. In this
regard, the straight-line or the declining-balance methods are commonly
applied. Yet, differences in rates are considerably large.

    b. Accordingly, key differences between the proposed Council Directive and
national tax practices arise with respect to the pool depreciation method
for tangible assets with a useful life of 15 years or less (short-term tangible
assets). Only Denmark, Finland, Latvia and the United Kingdom currently
follow a similar approach. In this regard, it is also worth noting that due to
the comparatively high depreciation rate of 25%, the proposed Council
Directive tends to be more generous for short-term tangible assets than
depreciation regulations in most countries under consideration.

(11) Exceptional depreciation is limited to non-depreciable assets that have permanently decreased in value and are taxed upon disposal under the proposed
Council Directive. While prevailing tax accounting practice is heterogeneous
in this regard, the strict limitation to non-depreciable assets under the proposed Council Directive cannot be justified from an economic point of view
as it places excessive limits on the deduction of actual losses.

(12) The list of non-deductible expenses provided for in Article 14 (1) of the proposed Council Directive illustrates common tax legislation in most countries

under consideration and seems to be accurate. In detail, non-deductible expenses may be classified in four different categories.

a. The first category includes profit distributions, repayments of debt and expenditures incurred for the benefits of shareholders. As the non-deductibility of these expenses follows commonly accepted principles of accounting and taxation, it is not only accepted under the proposed Council Directive but also in all countries under consideration.

b. The second category of expenses consists of corporate income taxes and other local profit or non-profit taxes, which are all considered as non-deductible expenses under the proposed Council Directive. By contrast, the majority of countries under consideration allow the deduction of local income taxes and real estate taxes for corporate income tax purposes. Yet, the treatment of taxes as non-deductible expenses under the proposed Council Directive has to be seen in the overall context of the proposal. Rather than allowing all local and real estate taxes to be deducted from the (consolidated) tax base, local taxes might be deducted after the common (consolidated) tax base has been allocated to the respective Member States, thereby preventing an undesired impact on the apportionment of the CCCTB for Member States that do not levy local taxes. Therefore, Member States could keep up their prevailing regulations if only a harmonised tax base (CCTB) would be introduced.

c. The third category covers expenses that are classified as (partially) non-deductible expenses, even though they may be incurred with a view to obtain or secure business income. Most important, Article 14 (1) (g) provides that those costs incurred by a company for the purpose of deriving tax exempt income (e.g. dividends received, proceeds from the disposal of shares) are non-deductible. In this regard, the majority of the countries under consideration are in line with the proposed Council Directive.

d. The fourth category introduces special regulations for the deductibility of interest expenses. In this respect, it is worth mentioning that the regulations provided for in Article 81 are far less restrictive than thin-capitalisation regulations in the 27 EU Member States, Switzerland and the US.

(13) The proposed Council Directive does not distinguish between gains and losses as ordinary or capital. All losses may be carried forward indefinitely to offset future income, but there is no carryback of losses to previous tax years. Moreover, so-called minimum tax regulations, which limit the offset of losses to certain thresholds or guarantee a minimum tax payment even in case of losses, do not apply under the proposed Council Directive. While we obviously find differences in detail (e.g. carryforward period), the tax loss set-off regulations under the proposed Council Directive are, in general terms, in line with prevailing tax practice in the Member States, Switzerland and the US. Only with regard to the forfeiture of loss carryforwards in case of changes in ownership or activity, the proposed Council Directive tends to be less restrictive than most countries under consideration.

To conclude, the results of the international comparison reveal that the majority of differences between the regulations for the determination of taxable income under the proposed Council Directive and current international tax practice are of minor importance. Moreover, considering the 52 different elements of the proposed Council Directive that have been analysed in detail, most deviations from prevailing tax practice are of formal or technical nature and are therefore expected to have insignificant impacts on the actual amount of taxable income. However, significant and substantial differences are identified with regard to the recognition and measurement of provisions, depreciation rates and methods, capital gains taxation as well as the tax relief for losses. Considering these results, we are convinced that the CCTB is appropriate to replace the existing determination of corporate taxable income under national tax accounting rules in the Member States. Further quantitative assessment on the impact of a CCTB on the effective tax burdens of corporations and tax revenue respectively is, however, still necessary to finally evaluate the proposal. In addition, some open questions remain that must be addressed in more detail once the proposed Council Directive is to be implemented into the tax law of the Member States. These open questions will be addressed in the following.

D.2. A Call for Clarity: Some Open Questions

The proposed Council Directive on a CCCTB provides a comprehensive and accurate framework for the determination of corporate taxable income within the EU Member States. In particular, the regulations on a Common Corporate Tax Base (CCTB) which have been analysed and compared in an international setting are coherent and do in many parts not deviate from prevailing Member States' tax practice.

Nevertheless, some open questions remain that have to be addressed in more detail once the Directive is to be implemented into the tax law of the Member States. Considering the first step of a CCCTB only, i.e. the determination of a CCTB without consolidation and formula apportionment, two categories of questions that raise practical concerns and – from our perspective – require further clarification in the ongoing evaluation process can be identified:

(1) Authoritative interpretation and regulations on the application of the more than 80 Articles of the proposed Council Directive dealing with the determination of a CCTB; and
(2) Achieving an Objective, Certain and Uniform Common Corporate Tax Base.

D.2.1. Authoritative Interpretation and Regulations on the Application of the Regulations of the Proposed Council Directive

If the proposed Council Directive should serve as an autonomous set of rules for the determination of a harmonised tax base across Member States, further regulations and authoritative interpretation appear to be necessary. Such regulations must provide comprehensive and detailed guidelines on the interpretation and application of the more than 80 Articles of the proposed Council Directive dealing with the determination of a Common Corporate Tax Base (CCTB). A default to national GAAP or national tax rules in matters where uniform treatment is not regulated in the proposed Council Directive – as one may infer from Article 7 – is undesirable and would jeopardise the overall objectives of a common tax base.

The basic principles underlying the determination of the tax base provided for in Article 9 of the proposed Council Directive (e.g. the realisation principle or the item-by-item principle) may not be sufficient enough to guarantee a common and uniform understanding of the general principles of tax accounting. Moreover, further guidance and detailed clarifications regarding certain legal definitions for the recognition (e.g. clear notions of assets and liabilities) and the measurement of revenue and expenses (e.g. precise definitions of the depreciation base or costs) need to be established. Finally, in order to assure a uniform application of the proposed Council Directive across Member States, clear legal concepts have to be provided for special areas of tax accounting, e.g. leasing arrangements.

Based on the analysis of the national tax accounting practice in the EU Member States, Switzerland and the US, Table 11 presents a non-exhaustive list of concerns about the practical application of the proposed Council Directive that require further consideration in the ongoing evaluation process. These concerns and open questions mainly cover transitional rules, comprehensive regulations for the interpretation and application of the regulations of the proposed Council Directive that govern the determination of taxable income and some details on the recognition and measurement of certain elements of the tax base.

Table 11: Open Questions Regarding the Interpretation of Selected Regulations of the Proposed Council Directive

Selected Issues of the Proposed Council Directive	Article	Open Question
Revenue		
Basic Principles Underlying the Determination of the Tax Base		
Autonomous Tax Law and Basic Principles Underlying the Determination of the Tax Base	Explanatory Memorandum / Article 9	As neither detailed rules nor authoritative interpretation is yet provided by the Commission, the application of the general principles, e.g. the item-by-item principle or the consistency requirement, might cause considerable difficulties and non-uniform treatment in the Member States.
Timing of Revenue		
General Principle (Accrual Principle / Realisation Principle)	Article 9 / 17 / 18	Given that the proposed Council Directive does not interfere with financial accounting regulations and considering that commercial law is not yet harmonised within the EU, questions arise with respect to the interpretation of the general regulations provided for in Article 9, 17 and 18. For example, the vague revenue timing criteria under Articles 17 and 18 are likely to yield non-uniform timing of revenues across Member States.

Selected Issues of the Proposed Council Directive	Article	Open Question
Exceptions from the General Realisation Principle		
Financial Assets and Liabilities held for Trading (Taxed)	Article 23	Without a formal link to financial accounting regulations several details regarding the application of Article 23 in practice remain open. Most important, common guidelines are missing on how the fair value of financial assets is to be determined when there is no active market.
Controlled Foreign Company (Applicable)	Article 82	Open questions remain in detail. For example, it remains undefined how the proposed Council Directive would deal with chains of controlled foreign companies in third countries. Most important, however, clear guidance on how to avoid international double taxation if CFC-income is included in the taxpayer's tax base is missing. In particular, it remains unclear whether a tax credit of any third country tax would be available under the double tax relief regulation of Article 76.
Exempt Revenue (Exempt Amount in Brackets)		
Profit Distributions (95%)	Article 11 (c)	It seems advisable to include a detailed definition of dividends qualifying for exemption. In particular, clear guidance on the treatment of deemed dividends is missing. A lack of detailed guidance remains also with respect to the switch-over rule of Article 73. Besides unclear definition (e.g. what regimes are considered special for purposes of articles 73) or several details on and computing the credit under Article 76, especially the relationship of existing tax treaties with third countries, although it is understood that such treaties will override the rules of the proposed Council Directive.
Income of a Permanent Establishment (100%)	Article 11 (e)	With regard to the treatment of foreign permanent establishments, common rules for defining the exempt income, i.e. the allocation of income to foreign permanent establishments, are still to be established. In addition, the proposed Council Directive remains silent on the treatment of losses incurred by foreign permanent establishments.
Deductible Expenses		
Stocks and Work-in-Progress		
Initial Measuremen (Direct Cost / Option to Include Indirect Cost)	Article 21 / 29 (2)	The definition of the initial cost of stocks and work-in-progress under Article 29 (2) provides only a rough idea of what is to be measured as costs of inventory. In particular, clarification is needed regarding the distinction between direct and indirect cost. Furthermore, an in-depth definition of individual cost components is required.

Selected Issues of the Proposed Council Directive	Article	Open Question
Initial Measurement (Direct Cost / Option to Include Indirect Cost)	Article 21 / 29 (2)	Clarification is also needed with respect to the option to include indirect costs. In this regard, solutions have to be established in order to ensure the administrative advantages of a harmonised and uniform tax base in the EU.
Subsequent Measurement (Lower of Cost and Market)	Article 29 (4)	Referring to the subsequent measurement of stock items, further regulations are necessary to ensure uniform interpretation of the term net-realisable value. In this respect, a legal definition of the terms "ordinary course of business" or "cost of completion" is recommended.
Bad Debt Receivables		
General and Specific Allowance (Permitted)	Article 27	Referring to bad debt receivables, further regulations are necessary to ensure uniform interpretation. In particular, clarification is needed with regard to the criteria to build general provisions, e.g. what qualifies as a large number of homogenous receivables and how to determine reliable estimates.
Provisions		
Provisions for Liabilities		
Recognition (Permitted, Legal Obligation)	Article 25 (1)	The recognition requirements, e.g. the minimum probability requirement (probability percentage), remain vague.
Measurement	Article 25 (2)	Similar to the question arising with respect to the minimum probability requirement, the measurement requirements, e.g. the kind of future developments taken into account when measuring provisions (inflation, salary increases), remain incomplete.
Provisions for Contingent Losses (Permitted)	Article 25 (1)	It is questionable whether contingent losses fall under the criteria of Article 25, i.e. whether contingent losses would be classified as obligations that arose from transactions carried out in the current or previous year.
Provision for Deferred Repair and Maintenance Costs (Prohibited)	Article 25 (1)	A controversial issue is the strict requirement of a legal obligation. From a mere economic perspective, provisions should also be admitted in case of constructive obligations, e.g. if there is an established pattern of past practice.
Pension Payments: Direct Pension Scheme		
Recognition (Permitted)	Article 25 / 26	As Article 26 refers to Article 25, the same questions regarding the recognition of other provisions arise.
Measurement	Article 26	Neither a particular technique for determining the pension provision is provided nor does the proposed Council Directive contain any specific information regarding the underlying determinants.

Selected Issues of the Proposed Council Directive	Article	Open Question
Other Deductible Items: Depreciation		
General Principles and Depreciation Base		
Entitlement to Depreciation (Economic Owner)	Article 34 / 4 (20)	Unresolved details remain with respect to the definition of the economic owner, especially with regard to proprietary rights, factoring, and leasing contracts.
Depreciation Base (Full Cost)	Article 33 (1)	An instruction for the key concept of an asset and many details with respect to the definition of the depreciation base / the depreciation amount are not provided (e.g. a clear distinction between direct and indirect costs or an in-depth definition of individual cost components).
Regular Depreciation		
Individually Depreciable Assets (Buildings, Acquired Intangibles, Machinery and Equipment (Useful Life > 15years))	Article 33 (1) / 36 (1)	No specific information regarding the determination of the useful life of assets is provided. It still needs to be defined whether the determination of the useful life of assets shall be based on the economical or technical lifetime of the assets.
Asset Pool (Machinery and Equipment (Useful Life ≤ 15years))	Article 39	In order to unambiguously determine whether the individual or the pool depreciation method is applicable, clarification, e.g. by a more precise description of different categories of fixed assets as designated by Article 42, is necessary.
Exceptional Depreciation		
Depreciable Assets (Prohibited)	Article 41	From a mere economic perspective, there is no justification to limit exceptional depreciation to non-depreciable assets. In particular, this holds true for depreciable assets which are depreciated on an individual basis (e.g. tangible fixed assets with a useful life of more than 15 years, buildings and acquired intangibles).
Selected Issues of the Proposed Council Directive	**Article**	**Open Question**
Depreciable Assets (Prohibited)	Article 41	In addition, in practice, the limitation is likely to force taxpayers to dispose depreciable assets but retain a beneficial interest in them in order to deduct losses immediately.
Assets not Subject to Depreciation (Permitted)	Article 41	There is a lack of clarity as to what constitutes a permanent decrease in value of non-depreciable assets.
Non-deductible Expenses		
General Principles and Categories	Article 14 (1) / 15	Article 14 (1) provides a comprehensive and detailed list of expenses classified as non-deductible expenses. This list illustrates common tax legislation in most Member States and seems to be accurate. Yet, it has to be kept in mind that the definition of certain terms (e.g. the exact definition of entertainment cost or bribes) might be interpreted differently within the Member States. Thus, further clarification of these terms seems to be necessary in order to guarantee uniform treatment in all Member States.

D.2.2. Achieving an Objective, Certain and Uniform Common Corporate Tax Base

Objectivity is a guiding principle of tax policy. In this regard, the proposed Council Directive provides a comprehensive and clear guideline for the main elements of the tax base. In order to achieve a common and harmonised application of tax accounting practice across Member States it is crucial to establish a mandatory system. Objective in this sense means that the CCTB has to be implemented without any tax accounting options for the taxpayer. In this regard, the regulations of Articles 21 and 29 dealing with the measurement of items of stock and work-in-progress conflict an objective and uniform taxation across Member States. In this regard, definite regulations are advisable.

By contrast, the prescription of an explicit discount rate for provisions and pension provisions is to be welcomed. Nevertheless, the application of a short-term discount rate, i.e. the Euribor for obligations with a maturity of 12 months, is questionable. Considering the long-term character of pensions, a long-term discount rate seems to be more appropriate. The same holds true for the depreciation of short-term tangible assets under the pooling approach. In this regard, the depreciation rate of 25% as provided by the proposed Council Directive tends to be much more generous than the depreciation regulations in most EU Member States.

Furthermore, it is important to note that special rules to deal with the differences between the proposed Council Directive and national tax accounting regulations are required to secure a smooth transition from national tax accounting to the proposed CCCTB. Moreover, these rules have to prevent that revenues and expenses are taxed or deducted twice and ensure that all assets and liabilities are recognised and measured uniformly in accordance to a single set of harmonised regulations. In this regard, Article 44 provides for a strict rollover of the existing tax book values. Accordingly, all assets and liabilities are recognised at their value according to the applicable national tax accounting regulations prior to applying the rules of the proposed Council Directive. Even though a revaluation to market value seems to be preferable in theory, the strict rollover of the existing tax book values appears to be the most workable solution. Not only would a revaluation to market value be costly and time-consuming, but it would also raise the question of how to tax any revaluation gain or loss (e.g. immediate taxation, taxation at a discounted tax rate or spreading the gain or loss over a number of years).

In order to ensure a uniform application of the proposed Council Directive once the assets and liabilities entered the CCCTB at tax book value, Articles 45-48 provide further adjustments. Obviously, the treatment of different depreciation rules and the treatment long-term contracts as governed by Articles 45 and 46 lead to a different timing in the recognition of expenses than under the national corporate tax law. Yet, both regulations provide simple and clear guidelines and are, in general terms, suitable to guarantee an objective and uniform application on transition to the proposed Council Directive. By contrast, open questions remain mainly with respect to the treatment of provisions (Article 47). In this respect, we may question how to handle differences that may arise in recognising and valuing such obligations, e.g. if the Euribor for obligations with a maturity of 12 months and the discounting rate applied under national corporate tax law differ. For these types of situations, we not only recommend to introduce more detailed transitional rules, but also to revise the general regulations for provisions as governed by Articles 25 and 26. Only if a comprehensive and accurate framework for the recognition and measurement of different types of provisions is provided, clear guidance on how to deal with differences between the proposed CCCTB and national regulations for provisions can be developed. Finally, it is worth mentioning that the national limitations on the tax loss carryforward remain applicable for losses incurred before entering the CCCTB under the proposed Council Directive (Article 48). Such coexistence of national and common loss relief rules causes considerable administrative difficulties and foils the idea of a harmonised tax base. From our perspective, all losses should, therefore, be eligible for an indefinite carryforward as provided by Article 43 (1) of the proposed Council Directive.

E. Summary of Conclusion

The main findings are summarised as follows:

(1) On March 16, 2011, the European Commission released a Draft Council Directive providing multinational companies with a Common Consolidated Corporate Tax Base (CCCTB) for their EU-wide activities.

(2) The CCCTB is a proposal to provide companies with the opportunity to determine taxable income at the level of each group member following a three-step approach: (1) Determination of individual income based on a harmonised set of tax accounting regulations, (2) consolidation of individual incomes and (3) allocation of the consolidated tax base by formula apportionment.

(3) As the second and the third step of a CCCTB, i.e. the consolidation and the allocation mechanism, still suffer from considerable shortcomings, we recommend introducing the CCCTB in two steps. The first step comprises the replacement of the national tax accounting regulations across Member States by a single set of harmonised tax rules. Such Common Corporate Tax Base (CCTB) would merely affect the calculation of the corporate tax base. Consolidation of individual incomes and the allocation of the consolidated tax base would, however, be omitted for the present and considered at a later stage of tax harmonisation in Europe.

(4) Our study contributes to the ongoing evaluation of the proposed Council Directive. For the first time, details on the determination of taxable income under the proposed Council Directive are compared to prevailing corporate tax accounting regulations as of January 1, 2011 in all 27 Member States, Switzerland and the US.

(5) The results of our study reveal that the majority of differences between the regulations for the determination of taxable income under the proposed Council Directive and current international tax practice are of minor importance. Moreover, many deviations from prevailing tax accounting practices are of formal or technical nature and are expected to have insignificant impacts on the actual amount of taxable income.

(6) Significant and substantial differences are identified with regard to capital gains taxation, the recognition and measurement of provisions, depreciation rates and methods as well as the tax relief for losses.

(7) Considering the results of the international comparison, we are convinced that a CCTB as established by the proposed Council Directive is appropriate to replace the existing rules for the determination of corporate taxable income governed by national tax accounting regulations in the Member States.

(8) Further quantitative assessment on the impact of a CCTB on the effective tax burdens of corporations and tax revenue respectively is necessary to finally evaluate the proposal. In addition, some open questions remain that have to be addressed in more detail once the proposed Council Directive is to be imple-

mented into the tax law of the Member States. These open questions mainly cover comprehensive regulations for the interpretation and application of the regulations of the proposed Council Directive governing the determination of taxable income. Moreover, clear legal concepts have to be established for special areas of tax accounting, e.g. leasing arrangements, in order to assure a uniform application of the proposed Council Directive across Member States.

Bibliography

Argúndez-Garzía, A. (2006), *The Delination and Apportionment of an EU Consolidated Tax Base for Multi-Jurisdictional Corporate Income Taxation: A Review of Issues and Options*, Taxation Papers, Brussels

Ault, H. J./Arnold, B. J. (2010), *Comparative Income Taxation. A Structural Analysis*, 3rd Edition, Alphen aan den Rijn

Avi-Yonah, R./ Benshalom, I. (2011), Formulary apportionment – myths and prospects : promoting better international tax policies by utilizing the misunderstood and under-theorized formulary alternative, *World Tax Journal*, pp. 371-398

Berry, C. H./Bradford, D. F./Hines, J. R. (1992), Arm's-Length Pricing: Some Economic Perspectives, *Tax Notes*, pp. 731-40

Bohn, A. (2010), *Zinsschranke und Alternativmodelle zur Beschränkung des steuerlichen Zinsabzugs*, Wiesbaden

Cerioni, L. (2011), The Commission's Proposal for a CCCTB Directive: Analysis and Comment, *Bulletin for International Taxation*, pp. 515-530

Commission of the European Communities (2001), Commission Staff Working Paper, *Company Taxation in the Internal Market*, SEC (2001) 1681, Brussels

Devereux, M. P. (2004), Debating Proposed Reforms of the Taxation of Corporate Income in the European Union, *International Tax and Public Finance*, pp. 71-89

Devereux, M. P./Loretz, S. (2008), The Impact of EU Formular Apportionment on Corporate Tax Revenues, *Fiscal Studies*, pp. 1-33

Devereux, M. P./Loretz, S. (2011), How would EU corporate tax reform affect US investment in Europe?, *NBER Working Paper No. 17576*

Dourado, A. P./de la Feria, R. (2008), *Thin Capitalization Rules in the Context of the CCCTB*, Oxford University Centre for Business Taxation Working Paper 08/04

Elschner, C. (2008), *Die Steuer- und Abgabenbelastung von grenzüberschreitenden Personalentsendungen*, ZEW Wirtschaftsanalysen 85, Baden-Baden

Endres, D./Oestreicher, A./Scheffler, W./Spengel, C. (2007), *The Determination of Corporate Taxable Income in the EU Member States*, Alphen aan den Rijn.

European Economic and Social Committee (2011), *Proposal for a Council Directive on a Common Consolidated Corporate Tax Base (CCCTB)*, ECO/302 CCCTB, Brussels

Freedman, J./Macdonald, G. (2008), The Tax Base for CCCTB: The Role of Principles, in: Lang, M./Pistone, P./Schuch, J./Staringer, C. (Eds.), *Common Consolidated Corporate Tax Base*, Vienna, pp. 219-270

Fuest, C. (2008), The European Commission's proposal for a common consolidated corporate tax base, *Oxford Review of Economic Policy*, pp. 720-739

Fuest, C./Hemmelgarn, T./Ramb, F. (2007), How would the Introduction of an EU-wide Formular Apportionment Affect the Size and the Distribution of the Corporate Tax Base? An Analyses based on German Multinationals, *International Tax and Public Finance*, pp. 605-629

Garcia, G. A. (2008), Deductible and non-deductible Expenses, in: Lang, M./Pistone, P./Schuch, J./Staringer, C. (Eds.), *Common Consolidated Corporate Tax Base*, Vienna, pp. 337-359

Hellerstein, W./McLure Jr., C. E. (2004), The European Commission's Report on Company Taxation: What the EU can learn from the Experience of the US States, *International Tax and Public Finance*, pp. 199-220

Herzig, N./Kuhr, J. (2011), Grundlagen der steuerlichen Gewinnermittlung nach dem GKKB-Richtlinienentwurf, *Der Betrieb*, pp. 2053-2058

Hohenwarter, D. (2008), Moving In and Out of a Group, in: Lang, M./Pistone, P./Schuch, J./Staringer, C. (Eds.), *Common Consolidated Corporate Tax Base*, Vienna, pp. 157-193

Jacobs, O. H. (2002), *Internationale Unternehmensbesteuerung*, 5th Edition, Munich

Jacobs, O. H./Endres, D./Spengel, C. (2011), *Internationale Unternehmensbesteuerung*, 7th Edition, Munich

Jacobs, O. H./Spengel, C./Schäfer, A. (2004), ICT and Profit Allocation within Multinational Groups, *Intertax*, pp. 268-283

Kahle, H./Schulz, S. (2011), Richtlinienentwurf für eine Gemeinsame konsolidierte Körperschaftsteuer-Bemessungsgrundlage in der Europäischen Union, *Steuer und Bilanzen*, pp. 296-303

Kahle, H./Schulz, S. (2011b), Harmonisierung der steuerlichen Gewinnermittlung in der Europäischen Union, *Betriebswirtschaftliche Forschung und Praxis*, pp. 455-475

Li, J. (2002), Global Profit Split: An Evolutionary Approach to International Income Allocation, *Canadian Tax Journal*, p. 823-883

Mclure Jr., C. E. (1984), Defining a Unitary Business: An Economist's View, in: McLure Jr., C. E. (Ed.), *The State Corporation Income Tax: Issues in Worldwide Unitary Combination*, Stanford, pp. 89-124

Mclure Jr., C. E./Weiner, J. M. (2000), Deciding Whether the European Union Should Adopt Formula Apportionment of Company Income, in: Cnossen, S. (Ed.), *Taxing Capital Income in the European Union: Issues and Options for Reform*, Oxford, pp. 243-292

Mintz, J. (2004), Corporate Tax Harmonisation in Europe, It's all About Compliance, *International Tax and Public Finance*, pp. 221-234

Mintz, J./Weiner, J. M. (2003), Exploring Formula Allocation for the European Union, *International Tax and Public Finance*, pp. 695-711

Newlon, T. S. (2000), Transfer Pricing and Income Shifting in Integrating Economies, in: Cnossen, S. (Ed.), *Taxing Capital Income in the European Union: Issues and Options for Reform*, Oxford, pp. 214-241

Oestreicher, A. (2000), *Konzern-Gewinnabgrenzung*, Munich

Oestreicher, A./Koch, R. (2011), The Revenue Consequences of Using a Common Consolidated Corporate Tax Base to Determine Taxable Income in the EU Member States, *FinanzArchiv*, pp. 64-102

Panayi, C. (2011), *The Common Consolidated Corporate Tax Base and the UK Tax System*, The Institute for Fiscal Studies, TLRC Discussion Paper No. 9, London

Oestreicher, A./Spengel, C. (2007), Tax Harmonisation in Europe: The Determination of Corporate Taxable Income in the EU Member States, *European Taxation*, pp. 437-451

Scheffler, W./Krebs, C. (2011), Bestimmung der Bemessungsgrundlage im Vergleich mit der Steuerbilanz nach EStG, *Deutsches Steuerrecht*, Beihefter zu Heft 22, pp. 13-28

Schön, W. (2004), International Accounting Standards – A "Starting Point" for a Common European Tax Base?, *European Taxation*, pp. 426-440

Schreiber, U. (2009), The Taxation of Hidden Reserves under the Common Consolidated Corporate Tax Base, *European Taxation*, pp. 84-91

Sørensen, P. B. (2004), Company Tax Reform in the European Union, *International Tax and Public Finance*, pp. 91-115

Spengel, C. (2003), International Accounting Standards, Tax Accounting and Effective Levels of Company Tax Burdens in the EU, *European Taxation*, pp. 253-266

Spengel, C. (2007), Common Corporate Consolidated Tax Base – Don't forget the tax rates!, *ECTR*, pp. 118-120

Spengel, C. (2008), Concept and Necessity of a Common Tax Base – an Academic Introduction, in: Schön, W./Schreiber, U./Spengel, C. (Eds.), *A Common Consolidated Corporate Tax Base for Europe – Eine einheitliche Körperschaftsteuerbemessungsgrundlage für Europa*, Heidelberg, pp. 1-47

Spengel, C./Malke, C. (2008), Comprehensive Tax Base or Residual Reference to GAAP or Domestic Tax Law?, in: Lang, M./Pistone, P./Schuch, J./Staringer, C. (Eds.), *Common Consolidated Corporate Tax Base*, Vienna, pp. 63-92

Spengel, C./Wendt, C. (2008), *A Common Consolidated Corporate Tax Base for Multinational Companies: some Issues and Options, Common Consolidated Corporate Tax Base*, Oxford University Centre for Business Taxation Working Paper 07/17, Oxford

Spengel, C./Zinn, B. (2011), Non-profit taxation on corporations in the EU: Lessons from corporate tax reforms in Germany and tax implications of the global economic crisis, *Intertax*, pp. 494-520

Weiner, J. M. (2005), *Formulary Apportionment and Group Taxation in the European Union: Insights from the United States and Canada*, European Commissions' Taxation Papers, Working Paper No. 8, Brussels

Zornoza, J./Báez, A. (2008), Definition of assets and capitalization problems for CCCTB purposes, in: Lang, M./Pistone, P./Schuch, J./Staringer, C. (Eds.), *Common Consolidated Corporate Tax Base*, Vienna, pp. 271-303